BIBLE STORIES
to
HEAR
and
TOUCH

Terry Jones

WESTBOW°
PRESS
A DIVISION OF THOMAS NELSON
& ZONDERVAN

Scriptures taken from the Holy Bible, New International Version®, NIV®. Copyright © 1973, 1978, 1984, 2011 by Biblica, Inc.™ Used by permission of Zondervan. All rights reserved worldwide. www.zondervan.com The "NIV" and "New International Version" are trademarks registered in the United States Patent and Trademark Office by Biblica, Inc.™ All rights reserved.

Scripture taken from the King James Version of the Bible.

WestBow Press books may be ordered through booksellers or by contacting:

WestBow Press
A Division of Thomas Nelson & Zondervan
1663 Liberty Drive
Bloomington, IN 47403
www.westbowpress.com
1 (866) 928-1240

ISBN: 978-1-4908-7457-9 (sc)
ISBN: 978-1-4908-7456-2 (e)

Library of Congress Control Number: 2015904722

Print information available on the last page.

WestBow Press rev. date: 04/21/2015

Contents

Dedication...ix

Acknowledgments...xi

Introduction..xiii

Introduction and History of the Old and New Testaments...................................... xv

Books of the Bible..xvii

The Old Testament 1

God's World Just for You: Genesis 1-2 3

Adam and Eve: Genesis 1:26–3:24.. 5

Cain and Abel: Genesis 4:1–16 8

Water Everywhere: Genesis 6–9 10

Tower of Confusion: Genesis 11 12

Abraham, Lot, and Salt: Genesis 13:1–13, 19:1–27 14

The Test: Genesis 18:9–15, 22:1–17...17

A Golden Ladder: Genesis 27–29 19

Joseph in Charge: Genesis 39–45 22

God Uses a Baby to Lead: Exodus 1–2 25

The Bush Speaks and Moses Questions: Exodus 2:11–23, 3:4–17, 4:1–18.........28

Let My People Go: Exodus 5:1–20, 7:14–24, 8–24 31

The Journey to the Mountain: Exodus 13–20...34

Balaam and the Talking Donkey: Numbers 22:1–35..38

Rahab: Joshua 2:1–24 41

Gideon: Judges 6–7...43

Ruth and Naomi: Ruth 1–4 46

Here I Am: 1 Samuel 1–3..49

A King for the Israelites: 1 Samuel 8–10 51

Anointed with Oil: 1 Samuel 16...53

David and Goliath: 1 Samuel 17 56

A Wish for a King: 1 Kings 3 59

Solomon's Temple: 1 Kings 5–7 62

Elijah and Ahab: 1 Kings 17–18 64

A Glowing Coal: Isaiah 6–9 67

Clay Pots: Jeremiah 18–20 70

Ezekiel and the Crowds: Ezekiel 4–5, 37 72

The Furnace and the Survivors: Daniel 1–3 75

Daniel in the Lions' Den: Daniel 6:1–28 78

Jonah and the Whale: Jonah 1–4 81

Birds of the Bible 85

Foods of the Bible 88

New Testament 93

A Blessing from God: Luke 1:5–25, 1:57–80 95

Another Miracle: Matthew 1:18–24; Luke 1:26–38, 2:1–20 97

Jesus as a Boy: Luke 2:41–51 100

Calling of the Disciples: Luke 5–6 102

A Wedding: John 2 104

John Baptizes Jesus: Matthew 3:1–17; Mark 1:9–11; Luke 3:1–3; John 1:32–34 106

Jesus Spoke and the People Listened: Matthew 5–6 109

Give Them Something to Eat: Mark 6:30–44, 8:1–9 114

Walking on Water: Matthew 14:22–33; John 6:16–24 119

Woman at the Well: John 4 122

Healing on the Sabbath: John 5 125

Jesus Speaks and the Waters Listen: Matthew 8:23–27; Mark 4:36–41;
   Luke 8:22–25 128

The Good Samaritan: Matthew 22:37–39; Luke 10:30–37 130

The Prodigal Son: Luke 15 132

Lazarus Come Forth: John 11:17–44 135

Palm Sunday: Matthew 21:1–11; Mark 11:1–10; Luke 19:28–38; John 12:12–15 138

The Last Supper: Luke 22; John 13 140

Dirty Feet: John 13:1–17 143

The Path to the Cross: Matthew 27; Mark 15; Luke 22–23; John 18–19 145

I Don't Know This Man: Matthew 26:31–75; Mark 14:27–28;
   Luke 22:30–34; John 18:25–27 148

Jesus Is Alive: Matthew 28; Mark 16; Luke 24; John 20 150

Doubting Thomas: Luke 24:36–38; John 20:19–29 153

Ascension: Luke 24:50–53; Acts 1:1–11, 2:14–16 156
Go Into All the World: Acts 1–2, 6–8 159

Additional Crafts and Activities 163
Additional Recipes 167
Glossary 171
Bibliography 177

Dedication

This book is dedicated to my husband, Henry, for his continual love and support. He taught me the true meaning of *Carpe diem,* Seize the day.

Acknowledgments

I am forever grateful to my husband, Dr. Henry M. Jones Jr., and children Julie Tipton, Sarah Mullins, and Hank Jones for their patience, support, and encouragement throughout my writing and research.

I owe a debt of gratitude also to Tammy Bell and Carolyn Steen for their technical advice they so readily supplied.

I give a very special thanks to Carolyn Campbell, Beverly Casteel, and Betsy Hutchison for the many hours of proofreading and content suggestions.

Introduction

As I was reading one of my many devotional books, one of my grandchildren asked me why I read such outdated books. The one I was holding was from 1985. I showed her my assortment ranging from 1936 to 2014. I held up my favorite, my Bible, with the cover taped in many places. "This is my favorite," I said. I explained the stories of God and Jesus and said that the advice and wisdom I received from the Bible would never become outdated.

Children today grow up in a time of computers and television. Most have iPads or smartphones that captivate their interests and time and give them instant feedback. Teaching needs to be adjusted to a shorter attention span with activities to illustrate lessons. Children are eager to learn but also want to be entertained.

This is a children's storybook written for the love of children and the need for them to hear and remember stories from the Bible. My goal is to make children want to read their Bibles for these stories and remember them. Children will hear with their ears but remember with their touch, and for that reason, crafts and activities are included with each story.

Remember as well to tell children facts relating to the stories, as descriptions of places, clothes, plants, and food. Introduce them to a loving and caring God who watches over them and loves them so much that He shared His only Son for them.

All these stories are short, and the craft projects are simple. Most supplies can be readily acquired at minimal cost.

Use this book along with your Bible to read the story, tell the story, and create the story.

—Terry Jones

Train a child in the way he should go, and when he is old he will not turn from it.

—Proverbs 22:6 NIV

Introduction and History of the Old and New Testaments

The Bible's sixty-six books were written by several authors inspired by God. It is divided into two sections, the Old Testament and the New Testament.

The Old Testament is the story of creation, genealogy, birth of a nation, laws for living, poetry, and other words of wisdom and prophesy. These stories span over 3,000 years. There are about 400 years between the Old and New Testaments.

The New Testament starts with the fulfillment of prophesies with the birth of Jesus Christ, God's only Son, and includes stories of His ministry, John the Baptist, miracles, and disciples.

After Jesus' death and resurrection, the gospel and teachings spread and the early Christian church was formed. The travels of Paul and other missionaries were written in the many letters to early churches. The ending of the New Testament is prophesied in the book of Revelation.

Books of the Bible

These books are divided into groups for easier memorizing. Encourage all children and leaders to learn them. This will always aid in Scripture reading and searching.

Old Testament

Law
- Genesis
- Exodus
- Leviticus
- Numbers
- Deuteronomy

History
- Joshua
- Judges
- Ruth
- 1 and 2 Samuel
- 1 and 2 Kings
- 1 and 2 Chronicles
- Ezra
- Nehemiah
- Esther

Poetry
- Job
- Psalms
- Proverbs
- Ecclesiastes
- Song of Songs

Prophecy

Isaiah

Jonah

Jeremiah

Micah

Lamentation

Nahum

Ezekiel

Habakkuk

Daniel

Zephaniah

Hosea

Haggai

Joel

Zechariah

Amos

Malachi

Obadiah

New Testament

Gospels

Matthew

Mark

Luke

John

History

Acts

Letters

Romans

1 and 2 Corinthians

Galatians

Philippians

Ephesians

Colossians

1 and 2 Thessalonians

1 and 2 Timothy

Titus

Philemon

Hebrews

James

1 and 2 Peter

1, 2, and 3 John

Jude

Prophecy
Revelation

Old Testament

God's World Just for You

Genesis 1-2

In the beginning was God. The world as we know was a huge, shapeless mass with no light or living creatures. It was in total darkness with vapors of moisture covering the entire surface.

On the first day, God separated the darkness into night and day. Day would be the source of all life. He was pleased. Knowing the world was covered with vapors, He separated them to make the top part sky. He had made day, night, and sky, completing the second day.

God realized the remaining vapors needed to be separated again; they became land and sea. All sorts of trees and vegetation grew on the land. The third day had ended.

God made a bright light and named it the sun, and the lesser light, the moon. In the heavens, He put all the stars that would brighten the night and also control the seasons—winter, spring, summer, and fall—all the seasons we enjoy today. This marked the end of the fourth day.

He made every type of fish and bird with the instructions to increase their number and populate the earth. That big job ended the fifth day of creation.

It was time to fill the land with animals and humans. Adam, who was made in the image of God, was the name given to the man, and Eve was the name given to the woman. He placed them in this beautiful world to have dominion over everything. God was well pleased and decided then that the next day would be one of rest. So on the seventh day He rested, making it our holy day, Sunday. God wants us to rest and honor Him. By resting, does that mean we should stay in bed all day?

God then had a new world with day, night, sky, land, oceans, trees, vegetation, sun, moon, stars, and animals—with the ultimate being man and woman. This new world was complete. God later gave Adam the job of naming all the animals.

Now close your eyes. We are going to imagine God making His creation. Remember, to experience this, you must keep your eyes closed.

Do you see total darkness?

Do you see the light or feel the heat from the light? (Shine a flashlight close to their faces.)

Do you feel the cool air? (Fan each child.)

Do you feel the vapors that made the ocean? (Mist each with a spray bottle.)

Questions

Where does the story of creation appear in the Bible? (Genesis)

What did God create first? (Night and day)

What day did God rest? (Seventh or Sunday)

Craft

Make sun catchers by painting with glass paints.

Instructions

Prior to meeting, remove the glass from five-by-seven-inch picture frames and cover the glass edges with masking tape. Give each child a piece of glass and a frame. Instruct them to place small drops of paint on the glass as the colors God may have used: brown for land, blue for sky, darker blue for water, green for trees and grass, and yellow for the sun and moon.

Paint can be applied in the order of days created or randomly, but emphasize using all the colors.

After the drops are on the glass, swirl to mix them with a paintbrush, but do not over mix them. All the areas should be covered. After it is completely dry, the glass can be displayed in the frame and hung as a sun catcher.

Supplies

Brown, green, light-blue, dark-blue, and yellow glass paint; five-by-seven-inch clear glass and frames, paintbrushes, cleanup supplies, and clear fishing line to be tied to the frame before inserting the glass to aid in hanging the sun catcher. Instruct the children to explain their colors in the way God used them when He created the world.

Adam and Eve

Genesis 1:26–3:24

God created a new world. In it lived Adam, a husband, and Eve, his wife, and every type of animal and plant. The Bible says God made Adam in His own image, so what does God look like? The place, the Garden of Eden, had many rivers, leafy trees, and animals of every kind. God had given Adam the job of naming all the animals and plants, so he was busy.

Life for Adam and Eve was good. They had a beautiful place to live and many things to eat, and they looked forward to daily walks with God. They had dominion over everything, but they had one rule to obey. God told them, "Eat of any tree you want, but not of the one in the center of the garden, the Tree of Knowledge of Good and Evil, for you will die."

One day, while Adam was busy naming things, Eve was alone. This is when the serpent or snake came up to her. This creature was very beautiful and cunning as he talked to Eve. He started asking questions. "Did God say you must not eat from any tree in the garden?" Eve told him they could eat from all except the one in the center of the garden. If they ate from that tree, they would die, she told the serpent. But he told her they wouldn't die if they ate the fruit of that tree but instead would have knowledge like God, knowing good from bad.

The more Eve listened and looked at the fruit, the more she was tempted. She wanted the fruit, especially if it would give her wisdom like God. She finally gave in and not only ate it but also convinced Adam to try some too.

This fruit was never identified as an apple in the Bible, but that is what most Bible stories name it. After eating the fruit, they looked at each other, realizing for the first time that they had no clothes on. They made clothes by sewing leaves together to cover their bodies.

Later, they heard God calling for them when He visited. They were frightened, and so they hid. Normally, they were excited when God came to the garden, but that time was different.

God asked, "Where are you?"

Adam answered, "We hid because we were naked."

God asked who had told them that. "Have you eaten from the tree I told you not to?"

Adam, quick to point the blame, said, "The woman you gave me brought some to me, and I ate it."

God was angry. When He questioned Eve, she told him of the serpent. Speaking to the serpent, God said he would be cursed and always crawl on the ground and be an enemy to all, especially women. Turning to Eve, He said she would give birth in pain and be ruled by her husband. He told Adam he would always have to work hard to survive.

God gave them some animal skins to wear and told them they had to leave the Garden of Eden. To keep them from returning, God placed a cherubim, an angel, in the garden with a flaming sword forbidding their entrance. They would go on living, but life would be difficult; instead of God providing everything for them, they would have to work just to live.

Questions

What did the Garden of Eden look like? (Beautiful, full of sunshine and smiling animals)

Who lived there? (Adam and Eve, with all the animals God had created)

Why were Adam and Eve kicked out? (They had eaten the forbidden fruit.)

Craft

Paint and name all the animals.

Instructions

Make believe you are God. You have created all the animals, but they don't have any colors. Remember, God gave the elephant his wrinkles and the leopard his spots, so any way you want to paint is okay. Design and paint your animal and give it a name.

Supplies

One pre-formed, plaster, small animal per child (which can be purchased at Walmart or a crafts store), acrylic paints of various colors, water jars, paintbrushes, paper plates, paper to protect tables, and paper towels for cleanup.

Optional

Color the sheet of Adam and Eve. Remind the children to choose colorful paint for the fruit and the snake.

Cain and Abel

Genesis 4:1–16

After Adam and Eve left the garden, they had two sons, Cain and Abel. Cain, the older, was a farmer who liked to stay close to home. Abel was a shepherd and had to go from place to place to follow his flocks. The brothers were very different in their actions, looks, and work.

Often, brothers can be jealous of each other, and this was the case with Cain and Abel. They both wanted to receive God's favor, and Adam and Eve had taught them that God wanted the best given to Him, so both brought offerings from their crops and flocks to sacrifice to Him and honor Him.

When it came time to offer a sacrifice to God, Abel killed his finest lamb and brought the best parts to be offered. Cain brought just some of his crop—and not even the best. God didn't find a difference between animal and plant sacrifice, but He did between "the best" and "just some." Although the Bible doesn't say why God accepted one and not the other, He favored Abel's sacrifice more than Cain's.

Cain realized this and got so mad that his face turned dark red with anger. When God asked him what was wrong, he didn't answer. He was mad at Abel for being favored by God, and he wanted to punish him. God told Cain that sin was waiting to attack him.

One day, Cain called his brother to the field, attacked and killed him, and buried him. When God asked Cain where Abel was, he asked God, "Am I my brother's keeper?" Of course, God knew what had happened. God told Cain he would be cursed and no longer get to farm and stay home but would instead have to wander forever from place to place.

Cain thought that leaving home as God said he had to would make him a fugitive and that someone might try to kill him. When he questioned God about this, God told him that if that ever happened, that person would be punished much worse than Cain was.

God put a mark on Cain, which would be a warning for others not to hurt him. We don't know what the mark was. Maybe it was like a tattoo. Cain had to leave his home, knowing he had failed God. His terrible mistake would remain with him forever, but God had spared his life. Cain moved somewhere else and became the father of many sons.

Questions

Who were the first sons of Adam and Eve? (Cain and Abel)

Why was God not pleased with the sacrifices? (God wanted the best.)

What did God do to Cain so people wouldn't kill him? (He put a mark on him.)

Craft

Put your "mark" on a mug so you will always know it belongs to you.

Instructions

Let each child design a personal glass mug. They can decorate them with permanent markers or ceramic or porcelain paint.

When they are finished, bake them in a 300-degree oven for thirty minutes to make them dishwasher safe. Some colors do fade and change colors, but they will be permanent.

Supplies

Permanent markers, porcelain or ceramic paint, glass mugs.

Water Everywhere

Genesis 6–9

God let Adam live a long time. Adam was 930 when he died, and his third son, Seth, was 912. Many descendants later, a man named Methuselah was born, and he lived for 969 years. Methuselah was the grandfather of Noah. Methuselah was known as the oldest man in the Bible.

God wasn't pleased with the world He had created. It was being filled with evil and violence, and many people turned from God. He decided to destroy the world and start over. In the midst of all these people, one family—Noah, his wife, his sons, and their wives, were good.

Perhaps the only water big enough to float a boat Noah had ever seen was a small river. God instructed Noah to build a huge boat, 450 feet long (one and a half football fields), 75 feet high, and 45 feet wide. God gave him specific instructions about how to build it. Don't you think Noah and his sons ever wondered if there would ever be a place it would float because it was so big?

Noah followed all the instructions, and God was pleased. Not wanting to totally destroy everything that had lived, God told Noah that the boat would hold Noah's family and two animals, male and female, of every kind. I'm sure Noah wondered how he and his sons would gather all these, but when the boat, now called an ark, was finished, the animals started coming by twos as God had directed them.

Finally, the doors of the ark were closed. The family and all the animals were secure. Noah was 600 when it started raining. For forty days and forty nights the rain came. Soon, no land could be seen anywhere, and the ark was floating. Water was everywhere. The Bible tells us, "Water covered the mountains to a depth of more than twenty feet." If you have ever seen a mountain, you can imagine how deep the water was. Everything except Noah, his family, and what animals they had with them was destroyed.

Noah and the animals were dry and secure as they floated around for seven months and finally stopped on Mount Ararat. Can you imagine the noise and smell that the family experienced? What about all the work of feeding and caring for the animals?

As the water started going down, Noah sent a dove out to see if there was dry ground. It would always come back since there was no place else for it to land. Every seven days, Noah sent a dove out. It had been over a year since they first entered the ark, but soon, it would be over.

Finally, the dove came back with an olive branch. Seven days later, he sent it out again, and that time, it did not return. Noah knew there was dry land because the dove had obviously found a place to stay.

God said to Noah, "Come out of the Ark; you and your wife, your sons and their wives, and all the animals … be fruitful and increase in number" (Genesis 8:16). As soon as he could, Noah built an altar and gave burnt offering to the Lord, thanking Him for their life and their safe voyage. God was pleased and made the promise that He would never again destroy the world with water. He placed a rainbow in the sky to show this promise. Noah, his family, and animals were safe. Soon, they would start raising new families.

Questions

Why did God destroy the earth? (The people were evil and did not worship God.)
How many people did He save? (Eight)
How long were they in the ark? (Over a year)

Craft

Make an ocean globe with the ark floating.

Instructions

Fill a bottle halfway with water and add a few drops of blue food coloring. Fill the rest of the bottle with cooking oil. Insert a small piece of wood to represent the ark. Seal and glue the lid. When it is turned from side to side, waves will form and the ark will ride the waves.

Supplies

One small jar per child, water, blue food coloring, cooking oil, one piece of wood per child, and glue.

Tower of Confusion

Genesis 11

After the fantastic voyage of Noah and the ark, for the next several years, the population of the earth grew. Remember God had said, "Go forth and multiply." This is what had happened. People were everywhere.

There were so many in the area around Babylon that they decided to build a city to become their home. Before that time, many had "wandered" from place to place, never staying in one area very long. They planned to build a tower so high in Babylon that it would reach the clouds and they would be as mighty as God.

The people gathered mud and straw to make bricks. They shaped them and put them in the sun to dry. Today in the Middle Eastern part of the world, where these people had lived, they still make bricks that way. Some made the bricks, others carried the bricks, and others built the tower with them. Everyone was working together.

The people were arrogant and proud. They knew their tower would make others in surrounding areas realize how smart they were and be envious. They thought that God would also be amazed. They felt powerful and thought nothing could stop them.

God looked down and saw them and was not pleased. He said, "They have forgotten me and think only of their importance. Soon, they will think they control everything, and nothing will stop them."

God was angry with them. He stopped them by giving each a different language. The ones who were making bricks still knew how to make them, but when they told the others where to take them, the others couldn't understand them. All who were working on the tower walked around babbling, which means talking but not being understood. No one knew what the other said. Everything was confusion; soon, the building stopped.

This would be the same if you visited another country, such as Germany or France. All around you, the people would be speaking another language. You could be tired and hungry, but you would be unable to make anyone understand. Soon though, you would find some who spoke English, and you would stay close to them, for they could understand you.

This is the same way it was in this city. People soon found others who spoke their language and gathered with them. They banded together and left the city. The building of their tower stopped, for there was no one left to complete the job.

This city was named Babel, meaning confusion. This was when God confused them by giving each group different languages. The Tower of Babel was never completed. There have been other great structures such as the pyramids, but none were as great as this tower would have been.

The people thought they didn't need God, because they had grown smarter than Him, but that soon changed. Maybe the lesson of the Tower of Babel is, "You need God to succeed."

Questions

What were they building? (A tower to heaven)

Why did they want the tower? (To be mighty as God)

What happened to the tower and the people? (God gave them different languages so they couldn't understand each other.)

Craft or activity

Build a tower or play the game Jenga.

Instructions

Work in groups of two or three depending on supplies. One game to use is Jenga, or any other type that has blocks. See who can build the tallest tower with each placing blocks. Tell them that when they get it built, another teacher will come in and give them further instructions. Have a Spanish-speaking or another language person come in with instructions. As the children still try to do their way, have this person say, "No," and knock it partly down, pick up a block, speak a lot of words, and hand the block to the child.

Lesson

Did you understand the second part of the instructions? This is just the way the people of Babel felt.

If time permits, play Jenga the correct way by taking turns to remove one block at a time until it falls. Everyone helps clean up.

Supplies

Several Jenga games or other building kits.

Abraham, Lot, and Salt

Genesis 13:1–13, 19:1–27

God told Abraham to leave his father's house and go to a land He would show him. The journey took Abraham, his nephew Lot, their families, and their flocks to an area around Bethel.

Abraham and Lot had great wealth and many animals. As the flocks grew, there wasn't enough grazing land for all the animals. Abraham said to Lot, "Look around, choose whatever land you want, take your family and herds and go there." Lot did that. He saw the cities of Sodom and Gomorrah and the beautiful valley so rich and fertile that there would always be grass for his herds. He chose the best land, leaving Abraham the wilderness to the west.

Both men settled in their areas, but Lot's family soon was surrounded by the sins of the city. The people in Sodom were wicked. They sinned against God by doing every bad thing possible. Lot's family remained loyal to God, but their neighbors did not.

Abraham had heard about the area where Lot's family lived. One day while sitting alone, the Lord appeared to him with two angels. They were on their way to Sodom and Gomorrah. Abraham recognized the Lord and had a conversation with Him. During this time, Abraham was told that when the Lord appeared the next year, Sarah would give birth to a son. Sarah heard this and laughed out loud because she was old.

Abraham told his servants to bring food for the men and water to wash their feet. After they had eaten, they rose to be on their way. While walking with them, the Lord spoke to Abraham alone, for the others had gone on ahead. Abraham knew the plan. God was going to destroy the cities of Sodom and Gomorrah because they were so wicked.

Abraham asked God that if He found fifty good people, would He still destroy the cities.

The Lord said, "For fifty, I would spare the cities."

Then Abraham asked, "Would you destroy them if there were forty-five righteous?"

The Lord said, "If I found forty-five, I would not destroy the cities."

Once again, Abraham was brave. "What if forty were found there?"

The Lord answered that they would be spared if He found forty.

Abraham asked, "What about thirty?"

The Lord answered, "I would not do it if I found thirty there."

Abraham was very brave, for then he asked about twenty and then ten, and the Lord said that if He found even those numbers, He would not destroy the cities. The Lord left, and Abraham returned home.

Questions

How many people did Abraham first ask for? (Fifty)

What was the final number? (Ten)

Would you have been brave enough to keep asking God these questions?

Chapter 19

When God sent the two angels to Sodom, Lot met them outside the city gates and insisted they stay with him and his family. As the wicked men of the city tried to break Lot's door, he pleaded with them. (To older children, you may want to explain why this was and the answer Lot gave according to the Bible verses, but not to younger ones.) The angels protected Lot and told him to get his family away from the city.

Early the next morning, the angels held the hands of everyone in Lot's family and led them through the city gates. Lot along with his wife and two daughters were safe. The angels told Lot, "Hurry, and don't look back."

Soon, Sodom and Gomorrah and all the surrounding area began to burn along with everyone in the city. Lot's wife was not obedient, for she had to see what was happening. She turned around to look and immediately turned into a pillar of salt.

This area is near the southern end of the Dead Sea. Do you know about the Dead Sea? It is called that because there is so much salt in the water that nothing can live in it.

(Demonstrate this by putting an egg in one cup of water and show how it sinks. Then dissolve a quarter-cup of salt in the water to show how the egg floats.)

If you were trying to swim in the Dead Sea, you would also float. All around the Dead Sea area are grotesque salt formations that remind all generations of Lot's wife and her disobedience.

Questions

Who was Lot's uncle? (Abraham)

Why did Lot choose this area? (It was the best land.)

What happened to Lot's wife when she disobeyed? (She turned to salt.)

Craft

Make a salt statue.

Instructions

Using packaged ice cream cones, cover with icing, and then roll in white or clear sugar crystals to represent Lot's wife. This is edible. You can use sea or ice cream salt, but this cannot be eaten.

Supplies

Ice cream cones, icing, sugar or salt crystals, plastic knifes, and plates.

The Test

Genesis 18:9–15, 22:1–17

God chose Abraham to become the father and leader of many people because Abraham was so faithful to God. God told him, "Look up to the heavens and count the stars … So shall your offspring be" (Genesis 15:5 NIV).

Many nights when he looked at all the stars, Abraham wondered how he could become the father of many nations, for he and his wife were old and had not been blessed with children. This is probably the same thought Sarah had, for she knew what Abraham had been told. Sarah decided to give Abraham descendants by giving him her maid, Hagar, and together, Hagar and Abraham had a son, Ishmael. Although Ishmael was greatly loved by Abraham, he was not the descendant God had promised Abraham.

God's promise to Abraham came true, for when he was a hundred years old, he and Sarah had a son. This child was named Isaac, which meant "laughter," for when Sarah had first heard the angel tell Abraham they would be parents even in their old age, she had laughed.

As Isaac grew, so did the love of Abraham for the Lord. God knew he loved him, but He decided to put Abraham to a test. God told him to take Isaac to a certain place on a mountain and sacrifice him. Isaac was his only son with Sarah, the love of his life. How could God ask this? Early, he had listened to Sarah and sent Ishmael and Hagar away. Abraham was wondering if God was punishing him for that.

He decided he would do what God had told him to do. He told his servants to gather wood and prepare for the trip. He would take Isaac with them to the mountain. Isaac was becoming a "man" and was excited about accompanying his father.

Abraham did not ask God any questions. He knew that human sacrifice had been practiced to worship pagan gods, but never to his God. But he had never questioned anything God said. He knew everything from Sodom and Gomorrah to the miracle birth of Isaac had come true, but he wondered why God had changed His mind. God had promised him many descendants, and Abraham knew they would be through Isaac, but how? Abraham was probably totally shocked at these words of God, but he obeyed.

When Abraham saw the place God had directed him to go to, he told his servants to stay while he and Isaac went farther up the mountain. He loaded the wood on Isaac's back, and he carried the knife and fire. They went alone. Finally along the way, Isaac said, "The fire and wood are here, but where is the lamb?" Isaac thought Abraham was going to sacrifice a lamb to God. Abraham told him, "God will provide."

When they reached the place, they prepared the altar. Abraham took Isaac, tied him up, and laid him on the altar. Isaac said nothing. As Abraham reached up with the knife to slay Isaac, the angel of the Lord said, "Abraham, do not lay a hand on the boy. I know you fear God, for you would have not withheld from me your son, your only son."

Abraham looked up and saw a ram caught in a bush by its horns. Abraham took Isaac off the altar and sacrificed the ram to God. Don't you think Abraham hugged Isaac several times that day?

The Lord was pleased and Abraham heard again, "I will surely bless you and make your descendants as numerous as the stars in the sky and the sand on the seashore" (Genesis 22:17 NIV).

In many of the synagogues, on festival days, the rabbi will blow the shofar, a ram's horn, to remind the people of the obedience and willingness of Abraham to obey God.

Questions

How many descendants would Abraham have? (As many as the stars and sands)
Who was Isaac? (The only son of Sarah and Abraham)
What did Abraham sacrifice? (A ram)

Craft

Make a water globe.

Instructions

Remove the lid from a jar. With some florist's clay, stick a small figure to represent Abraham on the center of the lid. Add water to the jar, stopping just at the rim. Add a half-teaspoon of glycerin and a teaspoon of glitter to the jar. Screw on the lid and caulk the rim with a hot glue gun. This will keep the water from seeping out. Flip it over and see how many descendants Abraham would have. (This can also be made without the glycerin using plain water.)

Supplies

One small jar per child, florist's clay, small plastic figures to represent Abraham, glycerin, water, and glitter.

A Golden Ladder

Genesis 27–29

Jacob and Esau were the sons of Isaac and the grandsons of Abraham. Esau was the oldest, and by the law, he was supposed to inherit the most from his father, but through the trickery of Jacob and his mother, Rebekah, that didn't happen.

Have you ever fought with your brother or sister? What happens when your parents step in? Usually they don't take sides, but not in this story. Rebekah favored Jacob, but since Esau was a hunter and always brought meat for Isaac, he favored him.

Isaac was getting old and going blind. He knew it was time to pass his inheritance in the form of a blessing to Esau, his firstborn son. Isaac told Esau to bring him some stew he had made and he would give him the blessing. Rebekah heard what Isaac had said and wanted the blessing for Jacob. She hurriedly made stew and took some of Esau's clothes. She told Jacob that she wanted to trick Isaac into thinking he was Esau and get the blessing. Jacob, however, didn't want to trick his father. He was worried his father would put a curse on him. Jacob also said that he had smooth skin, and Esau was hairy, so Isaac would know the difference even if his eyesight wasn't good.

But he finally agreed to what his mother wanted. Rebekah helped Jacob dress in Esau's clothes and tied some hairy goat skin to his neck and arms. Taking the stew, Jacob presented it to his father. Isaac reached out, touched Jacob's neck and arms, and smelled Esau's clothes. He gave Jacob the blessing that had rightfully belonged to Esau.

When Esau came in and realized what Jacob had done, he was mad. His brother had stolen his inheritance. Rebekah felt that Esau would seek revenge, so she convinced Isaac to send Jacob away to protect him. Isaac gave Jacob another blessing but told him to leave. He also said that when time came for Jacob to choose a wife and marry, Jacob should choose one of their own people, not a Canaanite. Esau heard this and was still angry at Jacob and his father. Do you know what he did? (He went out and married two Canaanite women.)

Jacob left and walked a long way. That night, as he made camp, he grew very sleepy. Finding a smooth rock to use as his pillow, he fell asleep and began to dream. In his dream, he saw a tall stairway that started on earth and reached all the way to heaven. At the top stood God. Up and down the stairs, angels were walking. Seeing angels in dreams was not uncommon for people in the Bible. Remember Mary and Joseph? People believed that angels were messengers from God. The Bible tells little about what angels really looked like, but artists usually draw them as glowing brightly with wings. However they looked, Jacob recognized them as special.

In his dream, Jacob heard God say, "I am Jehovah, the God of Abraham and your father Isaac. The ground you are on is yours. I will give it to you and to your descendants. For you will have as many as dust. They will cover the land from east to west and north to south, and the nations of the earth will be blessed through you and your descendants. I will go with you, protect you, and safely bring you back to this land." That was when God changed Jacob's name to Israel. All his descendants would be called Israelites.

When Jacob woke up, he remembered all of what God had said. Do you remember your dreams? (If time permits, have children tell some of their dreams.)

Jacob made the place where he was camping very special by making the stone he had used as a pillow into an altar. He named this place Bethel, which means "the House of God."

That day, Jacob began the journey that would take him to a new life that would include falling in love with a beautiful girl named Rachel. Jacob made a deal with her father to work for him for seven years to marry Rachel. But through her father's trickery, he first had to marry her sister, Leah. For fourteen years he had to work for their father to be able to marry Rachel. These ladies, their maids, and Jacob gave birth to sons who would become the leaders of the twelve tribes of Israel, God's chosen people.

Questions

Who were Jacob's father and grandfather? (Isaac and Abraham)

What did Jacob do to Esau? (He stole his birthright.)

Who are the Israelites? (God's chosen people, descendants of Jacob)

Craft

Paint rocks.

Instructions

Print the word "Bethel" or draw angels, ladders, or anything else that would remind them of the story. This rock can be placed under their pillows to help them sleep and dream at night. Talk about the coolness of the rock and why people often used them as pillows.

Supplies

One smooth rock per child, like a river rock large enough to paint, paints and paint brushes, water, and paper towels for cleanup.

Optional

Paint or color Jacob's dream.

Joseph in Charge

Genesis 39–45

Joseph was the eleventh child of Jacob but the first with his wife Rachel. Jacob favored him and his younger brother Benjamin the most. His older brothers knew he was special to Jacob and were jealous. Wearing a fancy coat that had bright colors, a gift from Jacob, Joseph would often strut around as if he were better than his brothers.

Many people in biblical times had dreams, and Joseph had many. In one dream, he saw himself as a ruler, with his brothers all bowing down before him. He told his brothers of that dream, and his attitude made his brothers resent him even more.

Later, all the brothers were in the field tending sheep when Joseph came to visit. They had made a plan to throw him down a well to get rid of him. When they saw a caravan heading for Egypt, they decided to sell Joseph as a slave to the people in the caravan instead. They took his colorful coat, the one Jacob had given him, and smeared it with blood, telling their father that wild animals had killed Joseph.

Times for Joseph were not as bad as his brothers thought they would be. Yes, he was sold as a slave in Egypt, but the man who bought him recognized him as special and hard working. Soon, he put him in charge of his other servants. Some things happened during this time, and Joseph was thrown into prison for things he had not done. Remember the dream of Jacob, his father, when he saw the ladder and the angels? God had told him He would protect Jacob and his family, and Joseph was his family. God would also protect Joseph while in Egypt. Although he was in prison, no harm came to him.

During that time, he interpreted dreams of the other prisoners and the guards. That was going to be the way he got out of prison, but he stayed there for many years.

Pharaoh was having bad dreams. Many of his advisors had tried to help, but they were unable to. Pharaoh heard of the wisdom of a prisoner named Joseph and how he had helped others, so he sent for him. He told Joseph that one dream concerned seven fat cows that were eaten by seven ugly, mean cows, and a stalk of grain with seven fat heads that were swallowed up by seven thin heads.

Joseph said that he couldn't interpret those dreams but that God would. The answer he received was that for seven years, Egypt would have a great abundance of food and then there would be seven years of famine with not enough to eat. Pharaoh was impressed and released Joseph from prison and put him in charge of government affairs to help prepare Egypt for the bad years that were coming. Joseph, once a slave, was given Pharaoh's ring and given an important position. That was when he would become the ruler of his brothers. Remember his earlier dream in which he saw them bowing down to him? That happened just as he dreamed.

Through the planning and wisdom of Joseph, Egypt saved up a lot of food and stored it while the people in other countries were starving and suffering. Jacob and his family were starving in Canaan and heard of the abundance in Egypt. He sent his sons to Egypt to buy grain. The brothers came before Joseph and wanted to buy food. They didn't recognize him, but Joseph recognized them. He sold them grain and asked if they had any other brothers at home. They told him about Benjamin. Joseph told them that if they came back to buy more food, they should bring Benjamin.

When the grain the brothers had bought in Egypt ran out, they decided to go to Egypt and buy more. They told Jacob what the ruler in Egypt had said about bringing Benjamin along. Jacob reluctantly sent Benjamin with them. He had already lost Joseph, but to save his people, he had to agree.

When Joseph saw Benjamin, he treated his brothers with a feast. When they prepared to leave with the grain, he hid a valuable, silver cup in Benjamin's sack. Only kings and noblemen used silver; everyone else used pottery.

On the way out of town, the brothers were stopped and searched. After a frantic search, the "prime minister's cup," which belonged to Joseph, was found in Benjamin's bag. Benjamin and his brothers were arrested.

Joseph told Benjamin, "You are guilty, so now you must be my slave." Judah, one of the oldest brothers, protested. He was the one who had originally convinced the brothers to sell Joseph in the first place, but that time, he told Joseph that he would stay in place of Benjamin for their father would die if he lost another special son. Remember that Benjamin was the son of Rachel and Jacob, Joseph's full brother. Judah made it clear he would sacrifice his life to save Benjamin.

That was when Joseph said, "Don't you see? It is me, Joseph. God sent me to rule Egypt so I could save you from starving!" Another dream was fulfilled. Joseph sent for Jacob and all the family to move to Egypt. The sons of Jacob became known as the twelve tribes of Israel and remained in Egypt for a long time.

Questions

Who was Joseph's father of Joseph? (Jacob)

Why was Joseph in Egypt? (He had been sold as a slave by his brothers.)

How did he trick his brothers? (He hid a silver cup in Benjamin's bag.)

Craft

Make a beaded bookmark representing the twelve sons of Jacob.

Instructions

Using about eighteen inches of cording, tie a Christian symbol or special bead representing Jacob with a double knot at one end. About ten inches from the Jacob symbol, tie another double knot. Thread ten beads representing the first ten sons of Jacob, but then for the eleventh bead, choose a larger and shinier bead to represent Joseph. End your bookmark with a less-shiny bead representing Benjamin.

Tie a double knot and trim excess cording. This is the twelve tribes of Israel bookmark. Children can learn the names of the each brother and his tribe at this time when they thread each bead: Reuben, Simeon, Levi, Judah, Issachar, Zebulun, Dan, Naphtali, Gad, Asher, Joseph, and Benjamin.

Supplies

Cording, a Christian symbol, and twelve beads, one being larger and shinier, and one not as shiny, for each child.

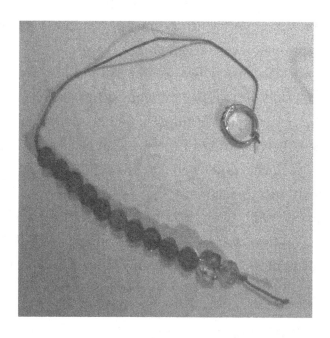

God Uses a Baby to Lead

Exodus 1–2

After the move to Egypt, Joseph and his family lived there many years. Their number became so great that the Pharaoh, who had never felt connected to this Israelite family, began to be worried that if he got into a war with a neighboring country, the Israelites, also called the Hebrews, might join the enemy. Pharaoh told the Hebrew midwives, who were the doctors, to kill the boy babies right when they were born. The midwives didn't do that because they feared God more than they feared Pharaoh.

At this time, there was a Hebrew couple who already had two children, Aaron and Miriam. When their third child, a boy, was born, they feared the law of Pharaoh and hid him as long as they could. When the baby was three months old, the mother had a plan. She made a big basket and covered it with tar to make it waterproof. She took the basket down to the river and placed her precious son in it. She told Miriam, the older sister, to hide near the reeds to watch.

This mother was wise. She knew that the princess and the other ladies of the court went to that place to take baths. Miriam stood very still, watching and waiting. When the baby started to cry, she didn't know what to do. The ladies were on their way, so she just quietly watched.

The princess heard the baby, saw the basket, and told her slave girl to go into the water to bring the basket to her. She saw the precious baby who was still crying when she picked him up. She knew it was a Hebrew boy, but that didn't matter. She planned to raise him as her son. Maybe he was for her like a forbidden toy.

Miriam, who was watching from the shore, bravely came up to the princess. "Do you want me to find a Hebrew woman to nurse this child?" The princess said yes. When Miriam returned with her mother, the princess handed the baby to his mother and told her to care of the baby and she would be paid. Miriam, her mother, and the princess were all happy. This baby would live. God was taking care of him.

Later, when the baby's mother brought him to the palace, the princess took him in her arms and named him "Moses" which means, "I drew him out of the water." The princess made sure Moses was raised and educated in the ways of royalty. Although he was born Hebrew, he was hers, and he was also an Egyptian.

Questions

Why was the baby put in a basket in the river? (To hide him from Pharaoh)
Who rescued him? (The Egyptian princess)
What name was he given? (Moses)

Craft

Enjoy an edible baby Moses

Instructions

Give each child two paper coffee filters, two Twinkie snack cakes, and selection of various colors of icing. Let them wrap their Moses in "blankets" of icing. Tell them to decorate both and eat one as snack but take the other home and tell their parents the story. Good to eat and fun to decorate. Send them home with a sugar high.

Supplies

Two Twinkies per child, plastic knives, various colored icing, coffee filters, paper plates, and cups of water to drink.

Optional

Color the picture of the baby with the princess.

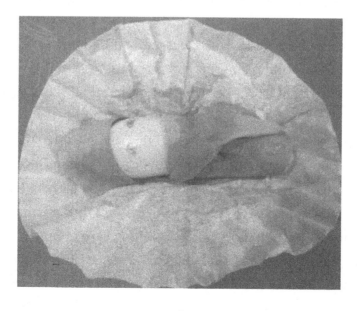

The Bush Speaks and Moses Questions

Exodus 2:11–23, 3:4–17, 4:1–18

As Moses grew up in the royal household, he was treated like the son of the princess, the grandson of Pharaoh. He was Hebrew but trained in all Egyptian ways. One day, when Moses was young, he saw a Hebrew man being mistreated. He intervened and ended up killing the Egyptian and hiding the body. That made him no longer a special person in Pharaoh's household, for he was wanted for murder. Moses ran and hid in the land of Midian for many years.

While in Midian, Moses put aside everything concerning Egypt. He married and became a shepherd. One day, while near a mountain called Mount Sinai, he experienced something unusual. In the middle of the field, Moses saw a bush completely on fire, but it was not burning up. He got closer to it and heard, "Take off your sandals, for the place where you are standing is holy ground. I am the God of Abraham, Isaac, and Jacob." Moses knew of this God and hid his face because he was afraid.

The Lord knew of the sufferings of His people in Egypt, and He was going to send Moses back to the land of his people. Moses questioned everything God told him. He was afraid not only of the Egyptians but also of his own people, the Hebrews. The Lord knew all of that. Moses had many excuses. No matter what the Lord said, Moses questioned Him. Finally, Moses said, "What if the Hebrews say you really didn't appear to me?"

The Lord told Moses to throw his shepherd's staff down. Moses did, and it became a snake, and Moses ran from it. The Lord told him to pick it up. When Moses did, it turned back into his staff.

The Lord told Moses to put his hand in his robe and then pull it out. When he did, it was covered with leprosy white as snow. Leprosy was a very contagious disease, and those who got it had to leave their people. God told Moses to put his hand back into the robe and pull it out again. Moses saw that it was healed of leprosy.

The Lord said that with these two signs, the people would believe. If they didn't, then Moses was to pour water into the Nile River and the river would turn to blood. The Lord thought those signs would convince the Israelites that Moses had been sent by God.

Moses listened but was still scared. His final excuse was, "Lord, I stammer when I talk." The Lord told him that He was the one who had given Moses his mouth.

Do you think God was getting tired of Moses' excuses? He told him He would teach him what to say.

One more time, Moses asked, "Lord please sends someone else to do this."

By this time, the Lord was angry at Moses and told him that Aaron, his older brother, would speak for him, and he was on his way. God said, "Take your staff, for with it you can perform miracles."

The bush went out. Moses had experienced a real conversation with God. Had he been courageous, or was he really a coward to question God? Moses soon headed toward Egypt, and on the way, he met his brother Aaron, just as God had said. He had to confront Pharaoh, but with the help of Aaron to speak and the will of God in his heart, he would be okay.

Questions

Where did Moses live as an adult? (In the land of Midian)

What did he see in a field? (A burning bush)

Why did he question God's plan? (He was afraid the people wouldn't listen to him.)

Craft

Color or embroider the picture of the burning bush. This is an activity that may take longer, so plan accordingly. During the next activity time, plan to retell the story explaining how Moses felt that he would not be able to do as the Lord had asked and had given God many excuses. What excuses do people give God today? How does God speak to people today?

Instructions

Use the template with the bush and words, "You are on holy ground." For older children, copy the picture to cloth for embroidery, but have younger children use paint.

Supplies

Burning bush template, one picture per child, crayons, markers, or embroidery thread and cloth.

"You are on Holy
Ground."

Let My People Go

Exodus 5:1–20, 7:14–24, 8–24

As Moses and his brother Aaron started their journey to Egypt, Moses remembered all the things God had said. He was still very nervous about facing Pharaoh, but he knew God would always be with him.

As they approached the camp of their people, the Israelites, the first thing he had to do was to convince his family, friends, and elders that he had been sent by God to help them obtain their freedom from the Egyptians. The elders didn't believe him, so Moses had to convince them that God had sent him. That was when he started doing the demonstrations that God had instructed him to do. He took his staff, threw it on the ground, and every one saw it become a snake. When he picked it up, it became a staff again. They still weren't convinced, so he put his hand in his cloak and pulled it out to show them the leprosy. He put it in his cloak again and pulled it out, and they saw he didn't have leprosy. They finally believed him. He told them that the Lord had seen their misery and wanted to help them.

Moses was eighty and Aaron eighty-three when they talked with Pharaoh. He refused to let the Israelites leave. He even made them work harder. Because they had to work more, the Israelites grew angry with Moses. The task God had given Moses was not going to be easy. He had to convince his people that he spoke for God and had to convince Pharaoh to let them go.

The Lord instructed Moses to go to Pharaoh and have Aaron put his staff on the ground. It would become a snake. Pharaoh was not convinced because his magicians were able to do the same thing with their staffs. Pharaoh's heart was hardened. Moses would have to do other things to convince him. These would be called the plagues that were put on Egypt by God.

First, he struck the water of the Nile River, and it turned to blood. Pharaoh wasn't convinced because his magicians, through their trickery, also made that happen.

Moses asked Pharaoh once again to let his people go. When Pharaoh refused, the Lord told Moses to have Aaron stretch out his hands over all the waters, and from it

31

came frogs that covered everything. Pharaoh begged Moses to stop this plague; Pharaoh promised to do anything Moses wanted, but when the frogs died, Pharaoh's heart was again hardened. So more plagues came.

So many gnats came that they clogged people's noses and mouths; they could barely breathe, but that didn't change Pharaoh's heart.

The fourth plague was flies that covered every man and animal. Pharaoh told Moses to take the people and to sacrifice to their Lord to ask Him to take these away. After the flies left, however, Pharaoh backed out on his word again.

The fifth plague killed all the Egyptians' livestock but spared all the Israelites' livestock. Still, Pharaoh didn't change his mind.

The sixth plague was boils, which are bad sores, that covered the Egyptians, but again, Pharaoh was unmoved. He wanted the Israelites to be his slaves.

The seventh plague was rain and hail that destroyed all the crops and damaged everything, even killing many people and animals that did not have shelter. That was when Pharaoh told Moses, "This time I have sinned. The Lord is in the right, and I and my people are in the wrong. Pray to your Lord and I will let you go. You don't have to stay longer" (Exodus 9:27–28). Moses stopped the rain and hail, but Pharaoh's heart was again hardened.

For the eighth plague, the skies were filled with locusts. They ate everything that the hail hadn't destroyed. Again, Pharaoh pleaded with Moses to call off the locusts and he would let the people go. When Moses did, Pharaoh changed his mind yet again.

Finally, for the ninth plague, the Lord caused darkness to cover all Egypt for three days. Pharaoh said, "Go. Take all your people, but leave your flocks and herds behind." Moses said they needed their animals for food and for sacrifices. By that time, Pharaoh was so angry with Moses that he told him to leave and if he ever saw him again, he would be killed.

Moses knew the final plague, the tenth, would be the worst. Approaching Pharaoh for the last time, he said, "The angel of death will pass through here at midnight. The firstborn from the highest to the lowest family will be killed. All Egyptian firstborns will be affected, and only the Israelite firstborn will be spared. You will beg us to leave."

The Israelites were preparing for the Feast of the New Year, one of their honored celebrations. In preparation, they were to take blood from the lambs they sacrificed and wipe it over the door frames of their houses. Moses said that would show the angel of death to "pass over" their house. He told the people to be ready to leave quickly.

When the final plague happened, crying could be heard everywhere. All Egyptian families experienced loss; especially Pharaoh, who lost his firstborn son, his pride and joy.

Pharaoh told Moses, "Go. Take your people, your flocks, everything." Moses told the people to leave fast; they weren't even to wait for their bread to rise. They Bible says, "There were about six hundred thousand on foot, besides women and children."

This was the end of the Israelites' 430 years of living in Egypt. A new way for God's chosen people was about to begin.

Questions

Who went with Moses to Pharaoh? (Aaron, his brother.)

How many plagues? Can you name some? (Ten: blood, frogs, gnats, flies, livestock dead, boils, hail, locusts, darkness, and death of the firstborn)

What does this last plague with the death of the firstborn have to do the word *Passover*? (The angel of death passed over the Israelite houses.)

Craft

Make a staff or a walking stick like Moses used.

Instructions

If possible, cut the stick of soft wood like privet hedge and have the children remove the bark. Another resource is garden sticks from Lowes or Home Depot. Have the children whittle or draw on them.

Supplies

One stick per child, table knife for removing bark or whittling, and markers.

The Journey to the Mountain

Exodus 13–20

Moses was leading the people away from Egypt. Excitement filled the air as they hurriedly walked toward a new home and life. God led them with a cloud they could follow by day and a pillar of fire at night.

Pharaoh soon realized the mistake he had made in letting all the Israelites leave. There would be no one left to work for him. He assembled his army and chariots to capture them and bring them back.

The Israelites saw the dust of the chariots that were coming after them and were afraid. The Egyptians were coming, and the Red Sea was in front of them. What were they to do? "Moses," they shouted, "why have you brought us to this place to die? It would have been better if we had stayed in Egypt." But Moses told them God would take care of them.

God told Moses to point his staff toward the sea and the water would part so they could walk on dry land. Moses did as God said, and soon, the water separated, and they saw great walls of water on either side of a path right through the sea. They hurriedly walked across. When the last group had crossed, they turned and saw the Egyptian chariots on the same path riding over the dry sea bed. But when the chariots got halfway across, the walls of water came down, and all the Egyptians drowned. The chase was over.

The Israelites, however, had to cross a desert, and soon they started grumbling again. They complained of never having enough food since they had left Egypt. Moses told them God would provide meat and bread daily, but he told them to eat only what they needed any one day. They were not to save any food.

Each night, just as Moses said, meat was provided, for the land was filled with quail. Each morning, the ground was covered with a sticky substance called manna that could be made into bread. They could eat all they wanted, but again, he warned them if they tried to save any until the next day, it would spoil.

After a while, they again complained, asking that time for water. The desert was dry, and there never seemed to be enough water for the people or their animals to drink.

God told Moses to strike a huge rock at Horeb and water would flow from it. God again provided what His people needed.

God instructed Moses to lead the people to Mount Sinai. They were to camp at the base of the mountain, and only Moses and Aaron could go to the top. Aaron did not go all the way up with Moses, for he was instructed to remain at a certain spot and Moses would go alone. For many days and nights, the people heard thunder and saw lighting up on the mountain. Moses was gone so long that they began to grow restless. Aaron had returned to camp, and the people convinced him to make an idol like the Egyptians had for them to worship. Aaron had them bring all their gold, and he melted it down and formed a golden calf. The people danced and partied around the calf.

When Moses returned with two stone tablets engraved with the laws God had given him, he saw the idol and the festivities. He was so angry that he threw the tablets at the calf, and the tablets broke into pieces. God punished all who were involved with the idol worshipping. God instructed Moses to again return to the mountain. When Moses descended that time, carrying new tablets, his face glowed so brightly that the people knew he had been in the presence of God.

Questions

What happened at the Red Sea? (The water opened up and they crossed on dry ground, but the Egyptians drowned.)

What did they eat? (Quail and manna)

What are the Ten Commandments? (Laws to live by)

Craft

Decorate a frame for the Ten Commandments document for the children's bedrooms.

Instructions

Let each child decorate a frame by using decoupage, jewels, paints, or stickers. Discuss the meanings of the Ten Commandments and why they should be followed.

Supplies

Template of Ten Commandments, art supplies including glue, jewels, and markers, and a document-sized frame for each child. Parchment paper works well for the Ten Commandment template.

Optional

Color the picture of Moses and the Ten Commandments.

The Ten Commandments

1. Thou shalt have no other gods before me.

2. Thou shalt not make unto thee any graven image.

3. Thou shalt not take the name of the Lord thy God in vain.

4. Remember the Sabbath day, to keep it holy.

5. Honor thy father and thy mother.

6. Thou shall not kill.

7. Thou shalt not commit adultery.

8. Thou shalt not steal.

9. Thou shalt not bear false witness against thy neighbor.

10. Thou shalt not covet.

Balaam and the Talking Donkey

Numbers 22:1–35

Do you remember the story in Exodus when all the Israelites left Egypt with Moses? Do you remember they traveled around for forty years? They weren't always in the desert or in an area where there were no people, for when the Israelites came to populated areas, the people there would fight them.

This story is about King Balak of Moab. He heard the Israelites were coming and got scared. Balak knew there were many Israelites. He described them as cattle that would lick the ground not making it suitable for any other animal. He knew of other areas where the Israelites had taken the land from the residents. Balak felt that with God's help, they could prevent the Israelites from taking their land. He sent for his sorcerer named Balaam, who was known to have a special connection with God. He wanted Balaam to ask God for protection and put a curse on the Israelites.

When messengers from the king approached Balaam, with the king's request, he said, "I will give you the answer the Lord says."

God asked Balaam, "Who are these people with you?"

Balaam said, "They are of Moab, and we want you to curse the people of Israel so they can be driven away."

God told Balaam not to go with the messengers and that there would be no curse, for the Israelites were His chosen people. Balaam sent the messengers away.

Another group of men came from the king and promised great riches to Balaam. He said again, "I will talk with God."

God told Balaam to go with them but say only what He told Balaam to say.

Balaam saddled his donkey and started off with them. He wasn't really obeying God; he was thinking about the riches they had promised him. God knew that and got angry. Balaam was riding his donkey on the road to the king's palace when the donkey suddenly stopped. In front of him was an angel with a drawn sword. The donkey saw the angel, but Balaam did not. When we talk of angels, we usually don't think about swords, do we? The donkey stopped and turned away. Balaam got mad and beat her and tried to get her on the right road again. Finally, they started off again. Again, the angel appeared and the donkey saw it. It started taking a narrow path and crushed Balaam's foot. Again, she was beaten.

The third time, they started off, and there again was the angel. The path was so narrow that the donkey could not turn around, so she just lay down. Balaam was really angry that time. He got off and beat her. How many beatings had she had? (Three) This is when he heard his donkey speak. "What have I done that make you beat me three times?" (Numbers 22:28 NIV).

Balaam said, "You have embarrassed me. If I had a sword, I would kill you right now."

The donkey replied, "Aren't I your donkey? Have I ever been in the habit of disobeying you?"

Balaam said no. That was when God opened Balaam's eyes, and he saw the angel in the road.

The angel asked Balaam, "Why are you beating your donkey? I came to warn you because you are wrong. She was protecting you by turning away."

Balaam realized he was wrong. He said, "I will turn back."

The angel replied, "No. Go with these men, but speak only what God tells you."

As the rest of the story goes, Balaam spoke with the Lord three times, each time following His directions, and he built seven altars for sacrifices, as was the tradition of the Israelites. Instead of God putting a curse on the Israelites, as the king had wanted, He blessed them. The king was furious, but Balaam realized he had spoken the real words of God.

Balaam had a tough time following God's voice. He needed something as stubborn as a donkey to open his eyes. Are we like Balaam?

Questions

Who was Balaam? (A sorcerer for King Balak)

What did the donkey see in the road? (An angel with a sword drawn)

Were the Israelites cursed by God? (No, they were blessed.)

Craft

Carve donkeys out of soap. This activity may take more than one lesson to complete.

Instructions

Prior to the meeting, purchase large bars of Ivory soap, one per child. Leave each bar unwrapped for twenty-four hours to dry and harden. Demonstrate scraping the

"Ivory" name off, and trace the outline of the donkey. Carve with a table knife, one not too sharp. Cut off small amounts at a time because trying to cut larger amounts may result in breakage. If this happens, alter the size of the donkey. Remind the children to take their time with this craft.

Supplies

One large bar of Ivory soap per child, donkey template, paper plate to carve into, table knifes, and a jar to hold soap scraps.

Rahab

Joshua 2:1–24

Joshua was with Moses and the Israelites for many years. When God told Joshua that he would lead the Israelites into the Promised Land, he was a little scared. He knew as they crossed the Jordan River that everywhere their feet touched would belong to the Israelites. Joshua told the Israelites to get ready for their departure.

"Be strong and have courage and do not be frightened. I am with you," God said.

The only thing He reminded them to do was always keep the laws that Moses had given them, especially the ones on the stone tablets, the Ten Commandments.

As they approached the area of Jericho, Joshua sent spies ahead to learn more about the city and the surrounding area. He reminded them that even though God was always with them, they had to be careful.

When they arrived in Jericho, they met a woman named Rahab. Rahab had known about the journey of the Israelites and thought they would take control of the city. She didn't have a good reputation, for she liked to entertain men. Do you think God uses only the best people for His work? Here was a woman others thought was a sinner, but she was the one God chose to help the spies by letting them stay at her house. God had led them to her place.

The king of Jericho heard of the approaching Israelites. He also had been told that strangers had entered the city and were at Rahab's house. He sent a message to her: "Bring out the men who have come to you. They have come just to take our land." Rahab didn't respond to the message.

The king sent soldiers to question Rahab. Opening the door, she said, "Yes, the men came to me, but I don't know where they were from. Before the gate of the city was closed, they left. Follow them quickly and maybe you can find them." Rahab lied to the soldiers.

Rahab had hidden the "spies" up on the roof of her house under some flax she was drying. Flax is a plant used to make linen cloth. After the soldiers left and the gates of the city were closed, she told the men, "I know of your God. I know what your people have done to the other lands you conquered. When our people heard the Israelites were coming, we were scared. Since I have helped you, will you deliver my family from death?" Rahab had a father, mother, and other family in the city.

The men answered, "Our life for yours! If you do not tell of our mission, we will deal kindly and faithfully with you when the Lord gives us this land."

She made a rope, perhaps out of flax the spies had hidden under, and let them down through her window to the outer side of the wall. She said, "Go toward the hill country. Hide for three days until your pursuers have gone home."

Before they left, the spies told her to gather all her family into her house and tie a red cord from the window. "Tell your family to stay in the house and they would be spared." The spies reminded her they could not protect her if she told on them. She immediately tied a red cord to the window.

When the men got back to Joshua after hiding for three days, they told him everything about Rahab and all that had happened in Jericho. They said the city was ready to seize. Entering the city, they immediately saw the red cord and saved Rahab and all her family.

Later, Rahab and her family were moved to a safer place. Rahab was a sinner in men's eyes, but she was used by God to give the Israelites the Promised Land.

Questions

Where were the Israelites going? (Across the Jordan River into the Promised Land)

Why did Joshua send spies? (To check out the land and the city)

Why did Rahab help them? (She knew of God and wanted to protect her family.)

Craft

Braid a small rope three cords using yarn or raffia, one being red.

Instructions

Give the children the cords. Tell them to tie a knot in the end and tape the knot to a table for ease in braiding. To braid, pull the right strand in front of the middle strand. Now pull the left strand in front of what is now the middle strand. Braid by always pulling the right over the middle and then the left over the middle.

Pull tightly while braiding, and when at the end, tie another knot. The red cord will be braided throughout. Tell them this is the way people made ropes, belts, etc. They can also make bracelets this way and add charms.

Supplies

Two strands of neutral-colored cord or raffia and one strand of red cord per child. Have additional supplies such as yarn or cording on hand to make other projects.

Gideon

Judges 6–7

The Israelites traveled for many years in the wilderness before they finally entered the Promised Land. With God's help, they had conquered many of their enemies, and life was good. They had food, homes, and most important, God, but all that would end. After they had lived there for a while, they began to be like their neighbors who worshipped idols, not God. Statues of Baal and other gods were all around them.

God knew it was time to teach them again that He was their only God. They were constantly being harassed by the Midianites. There had been no peace for seven years, and many Israelites were hiding in the mountains. They had no crops, no land, and no hope. Their only salvation was help from God.

A prophet, who was one who spoke the words God gave him, reminded the people about everything God had done for them. He said that God had brought them out of slavery and had given them that land, and he told them He was their God. They were not to worship anyone but Him. The people had turned away from God, who was not pleased about that.

God sent an angel to an Israelite named Gideon. The angel told Gideon that God was with them. Gideon asked that if God was with them, why they were being tortured by the Midianites. The angel said that Gideon was to save Israel. God would be with him.

Gideon told the angel that if that was true, he needed a miracle to prove God was really talking to him. Telling the angel to stay, Gideon immediately left and prepared a meal of roasted meat, bread, and broth. Returning, Gideon was told to put the food on a rock and pour the broth over the meat and bread, making everything soggy. The angel raised his staff, pointed at the rock, and immediately all the food was completely burned. Then the angel disappeared.

After seeing this, Gideon realized he had just talked with a messenger from God, and he was scared. He decided to listen to God's words from then on. God told him that when night came, he should tear down all the idols. He did as God said and hid in his

43

father's house. His father protected him and would not let the people take him. He told the people that if Baal wanted revenge, then Baal should seek it.

The Midianites were preparing to battle the Israelites. God told Gideon to gather as many fighting men as he could, and many thousands responded. But what the angel had told him about saving Israel still made him nervous. He would again put God to a test.

Gideon said to God, "If you are really going to use me, prove it this way. I will put wool on the floor, and if by morning, the wool is wet and the floor is dry, I will know you will help me." The next morning, Gideon walked on a dry floor, but he was able to squeeze out a bowl of water from the wool, which was very wet.

Gideon still wasn't convinced, so again he said to God, "Don't be angry, but one more test. This time, let the wool be dry but the floor wet." The next morning, the wool was dry but the floor was wet. Gideon was finally convinced. He knew God was on his side.

When God looked at all the men who had gathered, He said there were too many. God told Gideon to send home any of the men who were scared or didn't really want to fight. Twenty-two thousand left, leaving about ten thousand. God said that was still too many and instructed Gideon to take them to the river and watch them drink. Several put their weapons down and drank by bending down to the water, while others scooped the water into their hands, still looking around and being alert for the enemy. Those who bent down were sent home, leaving Gideon with only three hundred men. With just three hundred men left over from the twenty-two thousand, Gideon beat the Midianites.

In 1899, a group of men who called themselves "Gideon" started distributing Bibles to people. They put them in hospitals and hotel rooms, gave New Testaments to fifth graders, soldiers, medical staff, and college students. Every Bible or New Testament has the plan of salvation in the back in simple terms. The word of God is spread throughout many countries starting through this group of men. If you are in a hotel room, look for this Bible. (This is a good way to tell the children about the plan of salvation and how to ask Jesus into their hearts.)

Questions

Why was Gideon scared? (He was poor and from the smallest family.)

How many tests did Gideon use to question God? (Three)

Who first appeared before Gideon? (An angel)

Craft

The three tests from God.

Instructions

(1) In a pan, place bread and pour broth (water) over all and try to ignite it.

(2) Spread a piece of cloth on a table. Let child mist the area with water only on the cloth without getting any on the table.

(3) Spread a new cloth on table. This time, mist only the surrounding area without getting it on the cloth. Talk about the possibility of doing this and remind them that only God could succeed.

Snack

Have a bowl of trail mix. Have each child pick out thirty-two pieces and place on his or her plate. Then pass the bowl around again and tell them to put back twenty-two, leaving them with ten. Pass the bowl again and put back all but three. Remind them that that was how many men Gideon used to fight the enemy.

Pass the bowl around again and let the children enjoy the snack mix with additional water or juice to drink.

Supplies

Bread, water, cloth, mist bottles of water, bowls of snacks, paper plates, water or juice to drink, and matches.

Ruth and Naomi

Ruth 1–4

This is a love story that comes from the very short book of Ruth. It is how a stranger in Bethlehem had a very important role in the forming of our Christian history.

A man from Bethlehem left his country and traveled to Moab because there was no food for his family. With him were his wife, Naomi, and their two sons. Although the Moabite people were not readily accepted by the Hebrews, both sons fell in love with Moabite women and married them. This good life soon ended, however. The man and both his sons died, so Naomi and her daughters-in-law, Ruth and Orpah, were left alone with no husbands to support them.

Naomi decided to go home to Bethlehem. As she started the journey, she looked at her daughters-in-law and changed her mind. She told them they were both still young. She told them to stay with their people and the Lord would bless them with other husbands. She encouraged them to return to Moab to live among their people. Orpah, with tears in her eyes, bid Naomi good-bye and headed back to Moab.

Ruth, however, told Naomi, "Whither thou goest, I will go; and where thou lodgest, I will lodge; your people shall be my people and thou God my God." (Ruth 2:16 KJV)

Ruth would not leave Naomi. She spoke words of true devotion, and they are often used in marriage vows where the bride pledges herself to the groom.

Naomi and Ruth went to Bethlehem, where about a thousand years later, Jesus was born. When they got there, the farmers were harvesting their crops. Ruth knew that according to Jewish law, poor people could follow the reapers and gather any grain that fell to the ground. Ruth asked Naomi's permission to gather grain. Ruth left and went into the field of a neighbor, Boaz, a relative of Naomi's dead husband.

When Boaz was among the reapers, he noticed Ruth. He asked the foreman about her. He was told she was from Moab and had come back with Naomi after her husband and Naomi's son had died. Boaz was impressed with her devotion to Naomi. He told her to stay in his fields and follow his reapers, for she would be safe there. He told her that if she ever got thirsty, his workers would give her water.

Ruth asked, "How can you be so kind to me?"

Boaz answered that he knew of the love and devotion she had given to Naomi after the death of her husband and how she had left her homeland to live among strangers. Boaz asked God's blessing on her. He also asked his reapers to leave extra grain for her. God, through Boaz, was taking care of her.

When Ruth came home with a bushel of grain she had gathered, Naomi was shocked. Naomi asked her where she had been. Ruth told Naomi all about Boaz, how he had shared water and food with her, and how his reapers had left her extra grain. Naomi said that God was watching over them by providing all that grain. She told Ruth that Boaz was a distant relative.

Ruth told her that she planned to return to gather grain each day until the harvest was over. Naomi listened but warned her to do as Boaz said and stay in his fields, for she would be safe there.

As time passed, Boaz fell in love with Ruth. According to the tradition, a widow could be remarried to a close family member, and her land would become his, and their children would carry on the family name. First, before that could happen, Boaz had to talk with another relative who was more closely related to Ruth and had the chance to marry her first. That man said he already had a family, and he gave Boaz permission to marry Ruth. In earlier times in Israel, when a legal arrangement was made, the deal was finalized by taking off a sandal and giving it to the other person. This is what the kinsman did, thus making it official. Arrangements were made for the marriage and the purchase of Naomi's land.

Later on, Ruth and Boaz were blessed with a son they named Obed. Years later, he became the father of Jesse and the grandfather of King David. Many generations in the future, Jesus was born in the line of King David.

This is a story of a gentle, loving Moabite woman who was a stranger but played a very important role in fulfilling the promise of a Savior for God's people.

Questions

How many sons did Naomi have? (Two)

Why did Ruth go with Naomi? (She loved her.)

Where did Boaz first meet Ruth? (Grain fields)

Craft

Grinding grain into "flour."

Instructions

Give each child a bowl and about a third cup of bird seed and a rock. Have them grind the seed by crushing and rubbing it with the rock. Tell the children that this is very similar to the grain Ruth had harvested. The women would have to grind the grain to make the flour for their bread. Tell them that since this is birdseed and not grain, they will not use this for bread but will take it outside and scatter for the birds.

Give them snacks of crackers or multigrain bread dipped in honey. Tell them that today people are returning to eating whole grains because they are more nutritious. Any other snacks as oatmeal or any whole grains can be offered.

Supplies

A bowl and a rock for each child, bird seed, and snacks of bread, crackers, and honey.

Here I Am

1 Samuel 1–3

A woman named Hannah would often go to the temple to pray for a child. Hannah was old and had never been blessed with children. One day while she was there, Eli, a priest, saw her lips moving but heard no sound. He accused her of being drunk and corrected her. She told him she was petitioning God to give her a child; she wanted to dedicate him to the Lord. Eli told her to go and her wish would be granted.

Later, her son was born, and she named him Samuel. When he was very young, Hannah took him to the temple to live and serve the Lord with Eli, just as she had promised. Every year, she would bring clothes and visit Samuel. Eli raised Samuel in the temple as a servant of God.

Eli had two older sons. They should have been priests also, but they were evil. They took the sacrificial meat for themselves and did many other evil things. God was greatly displeased with them and told Eli they would not serve as priests in the temple. He would send someone else to take their place.

As Eli grew old, Samuel, who was about ten or twelve at that time, became one of his best helpers. One night while they were both asleep, Samuel heard his name being called and immediately ran to Eli. He said, "Here I am."

"I didn't call you," Eli replied. "Now go back to bed."

Samuel obeyed and soon again was asleep when he heard his name being called. Rising quickly, he went to Eli. Again, Eli said he hadn't called him and sent him back to bed.

A third time he heard his name. "Samuel, Samuel."

Again rising quickly, Samuel ran to Eli. He told him that he had woken up by hearing his name being called.

Eli immediately knew that Samuel had heard the Lord's voice, and that time, he replied, "Go and lie down, and if you hear the call again, say, 'Yes Lord, I'm listening.'"

Samuel went back to bed and soon fell asleep.

The voice woke him up again. "Samuel, Samuel."

He said, "Yes Lord, I'm listening."

Although Samuel was very young, the Lord told him all the things He had warned Eli about concerning his sons and how they would be punished.

When Eli woke the next morning, the first thing he asked Samuel if his name had been called again. Samuel did not want to tell him because he knew it was about Eli's sons. When he finally told Eli everything the Lord had said, Eli's response was, "Let Him do what He thinks is best."

As Samuel grew, God was with him, and the people listened as he spoke. He was becoming a prophet for the Lord. Samuel was called at a very young age to speak the words of God. Often times, God calls in our dreams.

Questions

Who was Samuel staying with? (Eli)

Why did he think Eli was calling him? (No one else was there but Eli.)

What did Eli tell him to do? (Go back to bed and answer the Lord.)

Craft

Make small pillows to represent Samuel being asleep when called.

Instructions

Stuff the pillow with fiber fill and show children how to sew it closed.

Supplies

One pre-sewn pillow per child with one edge open, fiber fill stuffing, needle, and thread.

A King for the Israelites

1 Samuel 8–10

Samuel was growing old. He had appointed his sons as judges, but they didn't always follow God. The elders were upset and told Samuel, "You are old. Your sons aren't like you. We want a king like the other nations." Until that time, the Israelites had been ruled by judges.

Samuel told God what the elders were saying. God said Samuel should listen to them. They weren't rejecting Samuel's ways but God's, which they had been doing since He had brought them out of Egypt. God wanted Samuel to warn them that having a king would not always be to their benefit.

Speaking to the elders, Samuel said, "A king will take your sons and daughters to serve him. He will take the best of the land, part of your food for his household, and you will become slaves for him. You will cry to God, but He will not listen."

The elders and the people said that didn't matter, they simply wanted a king who would lead them before each battle so they would be just like the other nations.

God said, "Give them a king!"

Later, God told Samuel that He would send a man from the tribe of Benjamin. He was to be the one anointed as leader for the people.

At that time, there was a young man named Saul. He had very good qualities and was very tall. Saul's father was from the tribe of Benjamin. Remember him? He was the twelfth son of Jacob and head of one of the smallest tribes. Saul's father had lost several donkeys and sent Saul and the servants to look for them. They went a long way from home, and finally, Saul felt they needed to return, for his father would be more worried about them than the donkeys.

The servant told him of a prophet named Samuel who might help them find the donkeys. Prophets were known for their wisdom. When Samuel saw Saul and his servants coming toward him, God said, "That is the one I told you about. He will rule my people."

Saul and the servants were invited to eat with Samuel and spend the night. He told them not to worry about the donkeys for they had been found. Saul was treated as a royal guest.

The next morning, Samuel took Saul aside and told him he had received a special message from God. He poured special oil on Saul's head, saying that the Lord had chosen Saul to be the king of His people.

Later, Samuel introduced Saul to each tribe and said, "This is the man God has chosen to be your king." Saul indeed looked like a king, for he stood a head taller than the other men.

The elders and the people responded, "Long live the king!"

Later, Saul led them into many battles and became the first king of Israel, obeying all the wishes of God.

Questions

What tribe was Saul from? (Benjamin)

Why did the people want a king? (To be like other nations)

What was Saul looking for when he went to Samuel? (Donkeys)

Craft

Make a crown for the first king of Israel.

Instructions

Using the corrugated cardboard like the edging for bulletin board borders, measure the size needed for each child's head. Cut the strip allowing extra for overlap to be glued or stapled. Decorate the outside to look like a crown with jewels, glitter, etc. Remind the children that this was the first king for the Israelites and to make it extra special. Staple edges closed and have children model their crowns and tell the story about Saul.

Supplies

Corrugated cardboard strip, glue, staples, jewels, stickers, paint, crayons, and other craft items to decorate their king's crown.

Anointed with Oil

1 Samuel 16

Saul, the king of Israel, was a very good leader. His army was victorious many times when he led them into battle. At first, Saul proved to be a bold and courageous leader. As the years progressed, though, Saul forgot that his power to win came from God, not from him. Saul was forgetting God.

In one battle, Saul captured a city with many sheep and cattle. God told him to destroy everything including the animals, but Saul didn't obey. He destroyed the people but sent all the animals back to his flocks and herds. Speaking through the prophet Samuel, God showed His anger. Samuel told Saul, "Since you turned away from God, He will turn away from you." Saul would remain as king, but he would be mentally tormented, and the Spirit of God would no longer be with him.

Samuel was then instructed to find a new leader for the Israelites. God instructed him to go to the area around Bethlehem to the home of a good man named Jesse. (Remember Jesse? He was the grandson of Ruth and Boaz.) God told Samuel He had chosen one of Jesse's eight sons to be the king to replace Saul. Seven men paraded before Samuel, and he was pleased. All were tall and handsome, and they had all the qualities a king should have. He prayed to God for wisdom to choose the correct one. God said, "Do not look at their faces, Samuel. God does not see the same as people see, for God looks at the heart."

Samuel asked Jesse if he had another son, and Jesse replied that David, the youngest, was out tending sheep. Samuel sent for him. David had the same features as his brothers, and Samuel immediately felt David would be the new king. Taking a flask of oil, he anointed David before his father and brothers and declared him to be the new king.

But David was young and had no ambition to be king. He was a shepherd and tended the sheep many long hours away from his home. He would pass the time by playing his harp, singing, and writing songs. David wrote many of the words in the book of Psalms in the Bible. David remained with his family for a while, but later, he was called to serve Saul.

The spirit of God had left Saul. He was tormented by many nightmares. Many people thought he was going crazy. Saul was desperate and would try anything. He had been told that music could soothe the spirit, so he sent his servants to find someone to bring music to the palace. One servant told him about the son of Jesse in the area of Bethlehem. This young man, David, played the harp, and perhaps Saul needed to hear David's music. Saul immediately sent gifts to Jesse and asked for David to come play for him. Saul was very pleased with David and sent a message to David's family telling them David would remain in the palace and service to Saul.

When Saul was troubled with nightmares, he sent for David, and David and his harp helped soothe him. A deep friendship developed between Saul, his son Jonathan, and David.

Questions

Why was God not pleased with Saul? (He forgot that God was the reason he was winning.)

Who was the next king? (David)

What did David do to ease Saul's pain? (He played his harp.)

Craft

Make a harp.

Instructions

Give each child twelve rubber bands of different sizes and a plastic container. The bands will become the strings, and the container the harp. Position the bands around the plastic container at even intervals. Different-sized bands make different sounds. Also, the tautness of the band affects the sound. Sing a simple song such as "Jesus Loves Me" with the children strumming their harps.

Supplies

One plastic box and twelve rubber bands per child.

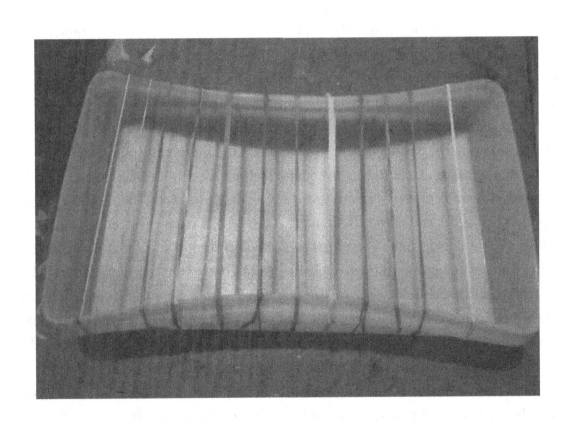

David and Goliath

1 Samuel 17

David, the son of Jesse, was a shepherd and the youngest of seven brothers who were all soldiers in the Israelite army. The army had been at battle with the Philistines for over a month. One day, Jesse called to David. "Take this bread and grain and check on your brothers at the camp where they are fighting." David obeyed his father. He found someone to tend his sheep and started toward his brothers' camp.

The Israelite army had been tormented twice a day by a Philistine giant named Goliath. Every day, the two armies faced each other and this giant would parade around, taunting the Israelites. Goliath was over nine feet tall, wore a bronze helmet, and had two hundred pounds of armor covering three-fourths of his body. There was a twenty-five pound ball at the end of the javelin he carried. Also, a soldier walked in front of him carrying a huge shield. Goliath was well protected. Everyone knew that if anyone tried fighting Goliath, Goliath would win. Goliath was too big for any normal man to fight.

Arriving at the camp, David saw the battlefield with both sides facing each other. He heard Goliath shout to the Israelites, "Do you need an army to settle this? Choose someone to represent you, and we will settle this in a single battle. If he wins, we will be your slaves, but if I win, you must be our slaves. Send me someone to fight!"

All the Israelite soldiers were frightened. Saul, the Israelite king, did not know what to do. He had offered a reward to anyone who would fight Goliath, but no one would accept the challenge. All the men were scared.

David asked some soldiers about the reward Saul had offered. They told him the person who killed Goliath would marry Saul's daughter and his family would never pay taxes.

David replied, "Who is this Philistine anyway that he can go against the armies of God?"

Eliab, David's oldest brother, heard David talking. "What are you doing here? What about the sheep you're supposed to be watching? Get out of here. You're just a brat wanting to see a battle."

David asked, "What have I done? I'm only asking questions." Doesn't that sound like two brothers talking?

Others heard David's questions and told Saul about him. Sending for David, Saul questioned him about facing the giant. David told Saul that he had killed many bears and lions that had attacked his sheep and that Goliath was no different. David finally convinced Saul he could beat Goliath. Saul had David fitted with armor from head to toe, but it was so heavy that David couldn't even walk. He took off his armor, went to a nearby stream, and carefully chose five small rocks. He said he was ready.

As both armies watched, David stepped out. Goliath laughed at the Israelites for sending just a boy. David put a rock in his sling and threw it at Goliath. This rock was not a small pebble; it could have been about the size of an egg. David knew he had one shot at Goliath. The rock hit Goliath in the forehead and knocked him down. David grabbed Goliath's sword and cut off the head of this giant of a man. The Philistines were scared. Their hero was dead. They ran away, and the Israelites chased them. The army of God had won with a young boy and a rock.

Questions

Who was David's father? (Jesse)

Why didn't David go to battle with his brothers? (He was too young.)

How did David kill Goliath? (Slingshot and rock)

Activity

"Kill" Goliath.

Instructions

On a table, place six plastic cups representing the Philistines and a twenty-ounce or larger bottle representing Goliath. Make a slingshot comparable to the one David may have used. Cut a rectangle five inches by two inches. Punch a hole in each short side. Cut two pieces of cording about twenty inches long. In one piece, tie a loop to place on finger, and tie the other end to the rectangle through the hole. This is the "retention" cord. Tie the other piece of cord through the other hole but with no finger loop, thus making it the "release" cord.

Place the "retention" cord over a finger, and with both cords together, twirl them overhead as if winding up to throw a baseball and releasing one cord. With practice, this can be done. Give each child five marshmallows representing David's five rocks and have them take turns throwing them at Goliath.

Supplies

Cording, rectangular cloth, six plastic cups, one twenty-ounce or larger plastic bottle, and marshmallows, five per child.

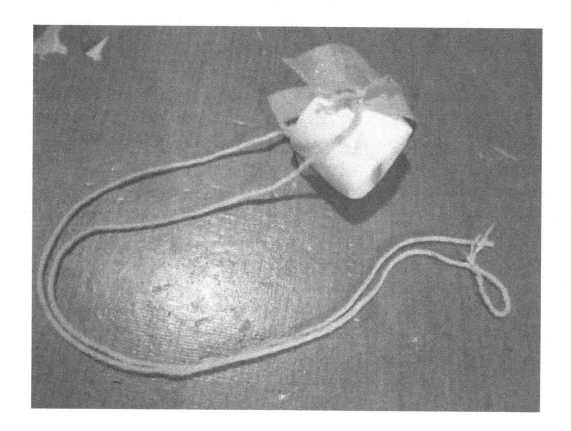

A Wish for a King

1 Kings 3

Solomon, the son of David and Bathsheba, became one of the greatest kings. David, his father, had ruled for over forty years and it came to be Solomon's time to be king. Later, Solomon carried out his father's dream of building a temple, but before that could happen, Solomon needed to grow as a king.

He offered many sacrifices to God. Since there was no specific place, the Bible says that he went to Gibbon, which had a tabernacle and ancient bronze altar where he offered a thousand burnt offerings. That pleased God. One night, in a dream, God appeared to Solomon and told him that He was pleased with Solomon and that if Solomon asked Him for anything, God would grant it. Solomon told the Lord that he felt like a child, not a king. He asked for a discerning heart, which means a person who listens and then makes wise decisions, and for wisdom to know right from wrong.

The Lord was pleased and told him that since he had asked for wisdom instead of riches or to rule over enemies, his request would be granted. The Lord told him he would be known for his wisdom and he would also have riches.

Solomon did have all this, just as the Lord said, and he used his wisdom to make difficult decisions many times. One was the time with a baby. There were two women who lived in the same house. Both had given birth to a baby at the same time, but one baby had died. The mother of the dead child took the other child as hers. Both claimed the child who was alive, and that was when the fight started. Soon, they were brought to Solomon to decide who got the baby.

The living child's mother told her side. The other one said, "No the dead child is yours and the living one mine" (1 Kings 3:22 NIV). Solomon gave the order, "Cut the living child in two and give each one half."

The real mother, probably with tears in her eyes, said, "Please my Lord, give her the living baby. Do not kill it."

The other mother said, "Neither one of us will get him. Cut him in two."

Solomon said, "Give the baby to the first woman. She is obviously the mother."

This is just one of the wise rulings Solomon made. God had answered his request and gave him wisdom to rule.

Solomon was known for speaking over three thousand proverbs, and he wrote more than a thousand songs (1 Kings 4:32). The book of Proverbs is divided into thirty-one chapters, and one can be read each day of the month. They are good teachings and advice from Solomon.

Questions

Who was Solomon's father? (David)

What did Solomon ask God for? (Wisdom and a discerning heart)

Who was the real mother of the baby? (The one who did not want Solomon to cut the baby in two)

Craft

Copy several proverbs from the book of Proverbs or elsewhere on paper or material so that the children can embroider or color it. Suggestions: "A soft answer turneth away wrath" or just proverbial sayings not necessarily from Solomon, such as "The hit you made yesterday won't win the game today."

Supplies

Cloth, embroidery thread, needles, sayings on paper, crayons, markers, or fabric paint pens. This activity may take more than one lesson.

Optional

Color or paint the picture of Solomon and the baby.

Solomon's Temple

1 Kings 5–7

David was about thirty when he became king. He wanted to make Jerusalem the capital city, and since it was on the top of a hill, it would become a fortress and superior to other places. Today, Jerusalem is a lot larger that it was in David's time. Then, you could have walked around it in about half an hour, but today, it covers about forty-one square miles and is populated by thousands.

David also wanted to build a permanent "church" or temple to worship God. God said no but told him to collect the finest wood, gold, and precious gems to use in the temple. His son, Solomon, would be the builder of this temple.

Solomon became king. It had been 480 years since the Israelites had left Egypt, and they needed a permanent place to worship. Solomon set out to do the task the Lord had planned, building a temple one hundred feet long, thirty-five feet wide, and three stories high. No building would equal it, and people from everywhere would marvel at its beauty.

He had 30,000 men as workers, 70,000 carriers, 80,000 stone cutters, and 3,300 other supervisors working for seven years to complete the job. Think of the prettiest and the largest building you have ever seen. Maybe it was a tall building with gold paint and furniture with jewels. That was how Solomon's temple would be. Remember, his father David had collected only the best materials for the temple. (Use a picture of large building to show the possible size of the temple.) The stone masons cut the huge stones and expertly fitted them together. The inside walls would be made of the finest wood with elaborate carvings all covered with gold. Outside of the holy inner room, guarding the doors, were two statues of fifteen-foot-tall angels. Can you picture the place now? No other structure was equal to this temple.

Questions

Who was Solomon's father? (David)

What did David collect for the temple? (Finest wood, jewels, etc.)

How long did it take to build? (Seven years)

Craft

Build a temple.

Instructions

You are Solomon and have designed it from the beginning. As David did for Solomon, you have all the supplies you will need to build it. Place the plastic box on the plate and start by "applying" the "glue" (the icing) to the walls of the box using the knives. Although the box is not edible, the decorations of this temple are. Be creative and have fun.

Supplies

Small, prewashed plastic boxes, one per child, icing, cookies, animal crackers, goldfish, gummies, or other edible items for decorating, a paper plate for holding the finished project, and table knife to spread icing. Think like a child and purchase items that you would like to use for decorating your temple. Have wet cloths available for cleanup.

Elijah and Ahab

1 Kings 17–18

Israel was ruled by an evil king named Ahab and his wife Jezebel. They worshipped the idol Baal, not God. Elijah was a prophet living near the king. A prophet was a person who was called by God to advise His people. Elijah would speak God's words, but they were often not what the people wanted to hear.

King Ahab had done more to anger God than all the kings of Israel before him. God sent Elijah to speak to Ahab. God was angry with Ahab and instructed Elijah to tell him that no dew or rain would fall for several years. Ahab would be angry at Elijah for hearing these words, so God told Elijah to go into hiding.

Elijah did as God instructed and left quickly. First, he camped by a stream and was fed by ravens, blackbirds, who brought him food. Then, following God's instructions, Elijah went to a city where a poor woman and her son lived. She had enough food for only her son and herself, but she graciously shared it with Elijah. Because she did that, Elijah told her they would never be hungry again, for there would always be flour and oil in her cupboard.

Elijah helped her later when her son, her only child, died. Through a miracle from God, Elijah brought him back to life.

Elijah had hidden for three years when God sent him to tell Ahab that it was going to rain. As Elijah stood before the king, Ahab realized this was the man he had been hunting for many years.

Ahab said, "So it's you, the man who brought this disaster on Israel." Elijah denied this, saying Ahab was talking about himself because his family worshipped Baal and not God. Elijah told him to bring all of Baal's prophets, 450 of them, and the other evil prophets, 400 of them, and come to Mount Carmel, which was the place the Israelites offered animal sacrifices to God.

Elijah told the people, "If the Lord is God, follow Him, but if Baal is your god, follow him." Elijah and Ahab would test their gods.

Elijah had Ahab bring a bull and make an altar but make no fire. Elijah said, "Call to your god of Baal and ask him to furnish the fire."

God then told Elijah to build his altar. So two altars but no fire were in front of Ahab and Elijah. Ahab prayed earnestly with his prophets all day and night, but no answer. Elijah listened and watched Ahab, and he told the Israelites to watch as well. Nothing happened at the altar of Ahab.

God instructed Elijah to take twelve stones, one for each tribe of Israel, and place them on the altar along with the bull, and then dig a trench. Next, God said to pour water all over the stones and the altar so that the water would run down into the trenches. This was done twice. Will anything that is soaking wet burn?

Elijah prayed to God, and fire immediately flashed down from heaven and burned up the wood, the stones, the bull, and even the dust. The people watched as the fire evaporated all the water that had been poured on the altar. They said Jehovah was God. Elijah told them to slay all the prophets of Baal and destroy their gods. How many prophets? (850)

God told Elijah to tell Ahab it was going to rain, and it finally did after three years. Jezebel, Ahab's wife, was so angry at Elijah for killing all her god's prophets that she promised to kill Elijah. Again, he went into hiding.

Questions

Who was Elijah? (A prophet from God)

What was Ahab's wife's name? (Jezebel)

Why didn't Elijah like Ahab and Jezebel? (They were evil and worshipped Baal.)

Activity

Fire demonstration outside in safe area.

Instructions

Let the children build an altar, placing wood, twelve stones, and the "bull" on it. Have one child pour water from the bottle all over the altar. Set it on fire. Say this is what the people of Israelite saw when Elijah demonstrated the power of God. The "water" is really lemon extract. You can tell the children if you desire.

Supplies

Wood for the altar, twelve stones, and "water" (lemon extract), marshmallow for the bull, and matches.

Optional

Coloring sheet of Elijah and the ravens.

A Glowing Coal

Isaiah 6–9

Isaiah was a prophet. What is a prophet? (A person who speaks for God.) This was a time when the kingdom of Israel had been divided and was about to be taken over by Assyria.

Isaiah was an educated man and could speak well. He would speak for the people and give advice that future generations would hear. When he was about twenty, while worshipping in the temple, he looked up and saw a vision of God on His throne. This vision was so large that God's robe filled the entire sanctuary of the temple. This was a vision that most people would never see. Six large seraphs were also with God. A seraph is a very unusual creature with six wings, a face, hands, and feet. The face looked like an eagle, and it had the body of a lion.

He saw two wings covering their faces and two covering their feet; they would fly with their last two wings. Can you picture this creature? Isaiah was scared. The seraphs began to sing, and their voices shook the temple. Suddenly, the temple was filled with smoke. Remember, when the Israelites looked at Mount Sinai when God was talking to Moses, it too was covered with smoke. This smoke covered the face of God from Moses and the people, but Isaiah had now seen God in this vision.

Picture Isaiah as a young man about twenty. Do you know a college student about that age? Isaiah had always tried to do right for God. He was minding his own business when he saw this vision of God and these huge birds. How would you feel? Scared? (Let the children respond with their reactions.)

Isaiah was scared. He thought he had done something bad and God was going to punish him. He said, "Woe to me, I am a sinner … I have looked upon the king."

One of the seraphs flew over to the altar and picked up a coal and touched Isaiah's lips. The seraph said, "Now you are pronounced 'not guilty' because this coal touched your lips. Your sins are forgiven."

Isaiah heard God ask, "Whom shall I send, and who will go for me?"

Isaiah immediately replied, "Here I am. Send me."

God accepted Isaiah as His messenger but warned him that the people wouldn't listen to his words. Later, Isaiah became one of the greater prophets, but just as God had told him, the people didn't listen to his words very often.

One of the things in the book of Isaiah was the prediction of the messianic child who would reestablish peace for a troubled land. He said, "For unto us a child is born; unto us a son is given; and the government shall be on his shoulder. These will be his royal titles; 'Wonderful,' 'Counselor,' 'the Mighty God,' 'the Everlasting Father,' and 'The Prince of Peace'" (Isaiah 9:6 KJV). Who was he talking about? (Jesus)

Here was a man, living over five hundred years before Jesus was born, predicting his birth. Isaiah was a mighty prophet, and his prophesies have been heard by many people, not only five hundred years later but even today.

Questions

What is a prophet? (A person chosen by God to tell His words)

How many wings does a seraph have? (Six)

Who is the Prince of Peace whom Isaiah talked about? (Jesus)

Craft

Two parts: demonstrate the burning feeling Isaiah must have felt to his lips with the coal, and using a charcoal pencil or a piece of charcoal, "paint" the picture of the seraph and Isaiah.

Instructions

Prior to the meeting, display a picture of a fireplace on the wall. Instruct the children to turn their chairs facing the fireplace. Tell them to stare at the fire and visualize Isaiah in the temple.

After a time, have them close their eyes. During this time, shine a heat lamp on each child's face. Still with their eyes closed, touch each child's lips with ice. This will "feel" like they have been burned. Talk about the feeling of coal on the lips of Isaiah. "Candy" coal is a good snack.

Optional

Color the picture of the seraph and Isaiah with charcoal pencils or a piece of burnt wood or charcoal. This is a different medium and may not have been experienced before by the children. Have paper towels available for blending and clean up. You may want to color one prior to meeting as example.

Supplies

Template of seraph picture, charcoal pencil or charcoal, ice cubes, optional heat lamp, and snacks.

Clay Pots

Jeremiah 18–20

Jeremiah was another prophet who lived in the last days of Judah, one of the lands of the Israelites. God had chosen him to become a prophet before he was born. When he was twenty-one, he started speaking for God, but people paid no attention to him.

The Lord instructed Jeremiah to go to the potter's workshop. There he would watch as the potter skillfully made clay pots, turning and molding them on his wheel. Soon, a pot or jar would appear as the potter gently worked the clay. Often though, looking at it, the potter was not pleased, so he squashed it and started over with a smooth ball he would turn into a perfect pot.

God told Jeremiah to tell the people that God was the potter and that Israel was the clay. He had built Israel into a strong nation, but they were doing evil things. If they didn't turn from their ways, He said He would crush them.

God told Jeremiah to purchase a pot and take the elders and priests out away from the city. Jeremiah bravely told them, "You have disobeyed God and worship false idols. You have done many evil things such as murdering and being greedy. God will punish you and break you into many pieces as this pot." Jeremiah threw the pot down, and it broke into too many pieces to be put back together. But even after that demonstration, Jeremiah's talk fell on deaf ears, and the people probably laughed at him.

Jeremiah continued to repeat the same message from God. The people still would not listen. They told him they weren't going to change their ways. They would live as they pleased, do what they wanted, and be stubborn and wicked. No matter how many times Jeremiah warned the people, they behaved badly. All throughout the book of Jeremiah are warnings to these people from God. They never changed, and at the end of the fifty-two chapters, the Babylonians destroyed Jerusalem and Israel just as Jeremiah had warned.

Questions

Who was Jeremiah? (A prophet)

Why was he warning the people? (They were evil and not following God.)

What did he do with the clay pot? (He smashed it to the ground.)

Craft

Make clay pots.

Instructions

Using commercial Play-Doh or salt dough (see recipe), have children form clay pots. Hold clay in hand and press in the middle with the thumb to make a hole. Continue shaping and pressing until the pot is the same thickness all around. Tell them that if they don't like the way it is being formed, they should start over just as the potter did. During this craft, have the children squash and restart at least once. They can inscribe their pots before they are set to dry. The salt dough can be oven or air dried and then painted.

Supplies

Play-Doh or salt dough, area for drying the pots, and paint.

Salt dough recipe

4 cups flour

1 cup salt

1 1/2 cups water

Mix and knead, adding more flour or water as needed.

Air dry or bake 300 degrees for about 1 hour.

Other recipes can be found at the end of this book.

Ezekiel and the Crowds

Ezekiel 4–5, 37

The Israelites had been captured by the Babylonians and forced to leave Jerusalem. Although they were captives, they still had some freedom and often worshipped idols as their neighbors did. Their captivity and exile lasted over sixty years.

Among the 8,000 exiles was Ezekiel, who served as a priest for seven years and then as a prophet for over twenty-two years. God told him he was to become the "watchman" for the House of Israel. God said, "Hear me and speak what I say to the people."

Ezekiel was ready to speak for God, but the people would not often listen to his words, so he had to find other ways to communicate his message. He did so by strange actions and demonstrations. The people often didn't understand what he was trying to tell them and thought of him as just an entertainer.

When they were asking about their return to Jerusalem, he took a piece of clay and drew a picture on it. Then, taking mounds of dirt, he made piles all around the clay picture. Next, he took a cooking vessel, like a skillet, and stood it on its end. The clay picture was Jerusalem, the mounds of dirt were the Babylonian tents surrounding Jerusalem, and the skillet was the wall forbidding their return. This demonstration was to tell the people that they would not return to their homeland.

Ezekiel demonstrated something else by asking for only water and barley bread. Only poor people ate bread made of barley flour. The water and bread represented hunger and poverty and a very slim diet. He never said much but used many demonstrations to illustrate the message from God. The people understood some of these demonstrations but didn't understood others.

He demonstrated what the fate of the people would be by shaving his head and beard and dividing the hair into three piles. These piles represented the people of Israel. One pile he burned, meaning that some of the people would be killed. He chopped up and scattered the second pile of hair, meaning some people would be separated from others and sent away, perhaps dying of starvation. The third pile he threw into the air. Some of the hairs stuck to his robe. This meant all the people would be scattered. The hairs that stuck to his robe meant that some people would be saved.

Ezekiel was a different prophet. Some people thought him crazy because of his actions, but they watched and listened. After many years, God sent a message that Israel would again be a strong. Their temple at Jerusalem had been burned, and they had been in captivity for a long time. They were beginning to lose hope. They needed to be revived.

God took Ezekiel to a place where the dead had been buried. As Ezekiel looked at those bones, God said, "Could these bones come to life again?" Ezekiel just looked; he didn't know how to answer that question.

God said, "Tell the bones I'm going to make them live again so they will know how powerful I am."

As soon as Ezekiel started speaking, there was a great rattling, and he saw bone coming to bone, and muscles and flesh forming on them. They became bodies, but they were not alive. God told Ezekiel to tell the winds to come from all four directions, north, south, east, and west, to blow and bring life to the bones. Ezekiel did as God directed, and before him were a vast army of people who had been formed from the bones.

The message was that Israel was going to be like these bones, all dried up and lost, but God would give them hope and would save them. He would put a spirit in them to make them strong and want to live again. The Lord would settle them in their own land. Then the people would know He was their God.

Ezekiel was a strange person, but he was a true prophet of God.

Questions

Why did Ezekiel demonstrate by actions the words of God instead of speaking them? (He would get the people's attention and they would listen.)

Who conquered the Israelites? (The Babylonians)

Name one demonstration that you especially liked. (Dry bones)

Craft

Make a man from both a paper skeleton puzzle and a plastic, preformed skeleton.

Instructions

Prior to the meeting, cut apart all the pieces of a purchased paper skeleton, making a puzzle. Time the children to see how long it takes them to put the skeleton back together. Hang it on the wall as reminder of the story of Ezekiel's message.

Give each child a plastic skeleton, Play-Doh, or salt dough and a paper plate. Show them how to take small pieces at a time and mold them over the skeleton to make a man. Remind them the part of the story how the bones, muscles, and skin came together. Let their "men" dry to be painted later.

Supplies

Plastic skeletons, one large paper skeleton for puzzle, Play-Doh or salt dough, paper plates, and paint for later. This is a good program for October, when paper and plastic skeletons will be readily available at party stores.

The Furnace and the Survivors

Daniel 1–3

King Nebuchadnezzar was the king of the Babylonians when the Israelites were conquered and moved from Jerusalem. He chose the brightest, most handsome, and most skilled young men to serve in his court. Among the chosen were Daniel, Hananiah, Mishael, and Azariah. Each was given Babylonian names. Daniel became known as Belteshazzar, and the others became Shadrach, Meshach, and Abednego.

For three years, they were taught Aramaic, as their language, science, and magic and were introduced to every type of knowledge available. These men received the best education and were offered the best food, the same food the king ate. Although they could have eaten the best Babylonian food, they chose to eat only vegetables and water because the king's food was high in calories and fat, not a diet they were accustomed to.

The king's servant did not want to let them eat only what they wanted for he feared they would look less healthy than the others and he would be punished. He finally agreed to give them ten days on their diets. At the end of those days, they were healthier than all the others who had eaten the king's rich diet. Remember that these men were Jewish and had been brought up with many dietary restrictions about what meat they could eat, so vegetables and water were their safe choices.

Daniel and his friends stood firm in their customs and worship of God although they were treated like Babylonians. King Nebuchadnezzar worshipped idols and wanted all his people to do the same. If they didn't follow his ways and worship his gods, he had them burned in a furnace. He knew that Daniel and his friends worshipped a different God, and although the king recognized their God, he would not worship Him.

Nebuchadnezzar had a huge, gold statue built that was ninety feet tall and ten feet wide. He invited all the officials to come to the dedication of this image. He made a law that anyone hearing music would fall down and worship this statue; if they didn't, they would be burned in the furnace.

The people obeyed; when they heard music, they stopped whatever they were doing, fell down, and worshipped his statue. Although most people did this, some refused. Do you know who? (Shadrach, Meshach, and Abednego, who would worship only their God.) The king was furious. He told them to worship his statue or be thrown into the furnace. Maybe their God would save them, but even if their God didn't save them, they would stand strong in their beliefs and refused to worship his statue his way.

Nebuchadnezzar got very mad. He had a furnace made, seven times hotter than normal, and he bound Shadrach, Meshach, and Abednego together. They were going to be thrown into the furnace. The heat of this furnace was so intense that the soldiers pushing them in were burned and killed.

Later, when Nebuchadnezzar looked into the furnace, expecting to see just ashes of the three, the king said, "Weren't there three? Now I see four, untied and walking around." He declared that the fourth must be an angel or the son of their God. He immediately had the door opened and summoned these men. "Shadrach, Meshach, and Abednego, servants of the Most High God, come out! Come here," Nebuchadnezzar said.

As the officials crowded around the three, they were amazed, for the men weren't burned at all, and neither was their clothing. They didn't even smell like fire or smoke.

The king declared that anyone who speaks against these three men's God, the one they trusted and worshipped who had just saved them, would be burned and their households destroyed. He said that no other god could save in that way. The king was so impressed with Shadrach, Meshach, and Abednego that he promoted them to higher positions in his kingdom.

Questions

Can you name the three men thrown into the furnace? (Shadrach, Meshach, and Abednego)

What did the king want his people to worship? (A huge gold statue)

Why did these men not obey the king? (They worshipped only God.)

Craft

Burn the three in the furnace.

Instructions

Have three children paint "men" features on rocks, while others make pipe cleaner men. After the men are made, and rocks painted, go *outside* and start a fire in a bucket. Throw all the rocks and pipe cleaner figures in and watch them until burned. Remind the children that the furnace that Nebuchadnezzar used was seven times hotter than usual. Put out fire and remove rocks carefully with tongs. The only thing burned will be the pipe cleaner figures, leaving only their wires.

Supplies

Three smooth rocks, twelve to eighteen pipe cleaners, bucket for fire, paper, and water to put fire out, matches, tongs to remove rocks, and towel to dry off.

Lesson

Rocks were made by God will survive just as Shadrach, Meshach, and Abednego had.

Daniel in the Lions' Den

Daniel 6:1–28

Daniel was one of the Israelites who had been taken captive when Jerusalem was attacked by the Babylonians. Daniel started out as a prisoner to the king and ended up as second in command. During his time of captivity, he always remained loyal to God and would worship only Him.

Daniel served under three kings—Nebuchadnezzar, Belshazzar, and Darius. King Belshazzar was so impressed with Daniel that he gave him purple robes and gold jewelry to wear, and he declared Daniel worthy of being the third highest ruler of his kingdom. That was not for long, however, for Belshazzar was killed and Darius became king.

Daniel was one of the 120 administrators Darius appointed to help him rule. Impressed with Daniel's leadership abilities, Darius placed him in a higher position than others. This appointment made the other administrators jealous, and they constantly sought ways to dishonor Daniel. They knew he would never break any of Darius's laws unless these laws went against Daniel's devotion to his God.

These rulers went to King Darius and asked him to make a law that anyone who prayed to any god or man except King Darius would be thrown into the lions' den. The rulers knew that if Darius made that law, it could not be changed. This was the way they planned to get rid of Daniel, because they knew he would go home, get on his knees, turn toward Jerusalem, and pray to his God three times a day.

The rulers found Daniel in his home praying and went to Darius. They first asked him about his new law, and Darius said the law could not be changed. They told Darius that Daniel was guilty of breaking the law because he prayed three times a day to his God. Daniel was Darius's favorite, and Darius tried hard to change the law but could not.

Darius told Daniel, "May your God whom you serve continually rescue you." Then they threw Daniel into the lions' den, which was a deep hole with a narrow opening, so there was no escape. A heavy rock was rolled over the opening. Darius and the other rulers placed their marks on the rock with the impression of their rings to officially seal the opening. Darius returned to his palace very upset. That night, he did not eat and wanted no company. He was sad because of what he had done to Daniel.

Early the next morning, he hurried to the lions' den and called, hoping Daniel would answer. "Daniel, servant of the living God, has your God, whom you serve always, been able to rescue you from the lions?"

Daniel said, "Oh King, live forever. My God sent his angel, and he shut the mouths of the lions. They did not hurt me because I was innocent and had done no wrong before you."

When Daniel was helped out, the king found no marks or wounds on him. He was safe. King Darius had the others who had accused Daniel, thrown into the lions' den, along with their families, and they were immediately killed.

Darius made another decree. "Every part of my kingdom must fear and revere the God of Daniel."

Daniel prospered under the reign of King Darius.

Questions

Why were the other rulers upset with Daniel? (They were jealous of him.)

Who was the king? (Darius)

What happened when Daniel was thrown into the den? (God's angel shut the mouths of the lions.)

Activity

Frost and eat lion-shaped sugar cookies.

Instructions

If time permits, give the children cookie dough and cutters and let them cut out and bake the cookies. Before they eat one, have them recite part of this story. Other purchased shaped cookies can be used, but suggest they use "lion" colors when icing them to better relate to the story.

Supplies

Cookies, frosting, knife for spreading, and paper plates.

Optional

Color the picture of Daniel and the lions.

Jonah and the Whale

Jonah 1–4

Jonah was a prophet, a man who spoke the words from God. He lived near Nazareth. God told Jonah to go to Nineveh, a large, wicked city with a population of more than 120,000 people. God wanted Jonah to tell the people they needed to change their ways or God would destroy the city.

Jonah was scared to travel to Nineveh and speak for God, so he boarded a ship for Tarshish. He went below decks to find a place to hide from God. Can a person really hide from God? Soon in this dark place, he was asleep.

Outside, the winds and the waves were rocking the ship violently. The sailors, fearing that the ship would sink, prayed to their gods and even started throwing cargo overboard to lighten the ship to save it. Jonah was still below asleep.

The captain woke up Jonah and said, "Get up and pray to your God to have mercy on us and save us." The crew had already decided that someone onboard was responsible for this weather and soon realized it was Jonah.

When they confronted Jonah, he confessed that he was running from God. The decision was made. Jonah had to leave the boat. Jonah said, "Throw me into the sea and all will become calm again." After trying hard to keep the boat afloat, they had no choice but to throw Jonah into the sea to save themselves. Immediately after they did this, the storm stopped. The sailors prayed to Jonah's God and vowed to serve Him.

But that wasn't the end of Jonah. God sent a huge fish, as tradition says, a whale that swallowed Jonah. He stayed in the belly of the whale for three days and nights, praising and thanking God for saving him. He vowed to always trust God and do what He asked.

The next thing Jonah knew, the whale spit him up, and he was on dry land. Again God told him, "Go to Nineveh and warn them of their impending doom." God was repeating what He had said earlier. This time, though, Jonah obeyed. Nineveh was so large that it would take three days to walk around it. Each day, Jonah would shout, "Forty days from now, Nineveh will be destroyed! Repent and turn from your evil ways."

The people believed Jonah, and even the king asked forgiveness from God. To show that they had repented, they changed from their festive clothes and fasted by not eating or drinking. The king issued a decree that all the people had to call on God and give up their evil ways. He told them to ask for God's compassion so their city would not perish.

God saw the entire city changing and decided not to destroy it. Jonah was angry. He told God he knew Nineveh would not be destroyed and he would look foolish because of the words he had spoken. Jonah was embarrassed and ready to die. God saved Jonah again from death and finally convinced him that the decision to save Nineveh was a good one.

Questions

Why did Jonah get on a boat? (He was trying to hide from God.)

What happened at sea? (Jonah was thrown overboard because of the storm.)

What happened to Nineveh? (Its people repented and were saved.)

Craft

Color the picture of Jonah inside the whale or make a whale pillow.

Instructions

Prior to the meeting, hang wet strips of cloth down from the door frame so children will feel as if they were entering the belly of the whale. Open sardine cans for smell.

For Pillow

Prior to class, draw a whale design on two layers of cloth. Sew all sides together except a small area at the bottom. Turn and press. Have each child stuff with fiber fill and sew opening closed.

This activity can be like "ring toss" with each child throwing a finished pillow into a basket or box representing the whale going back into the sea after "spitting" Jonah out on dry land.

Supplies

Picture template, crayons or paint, one whale pillow per child, needle and thread, and fiber fill.

Birds of the Bible

(Have pictures of birds to show when you tell stories)

The birds we see every day usually don't make us think of Bible stories, but when God created them, He had a plan for many different ones. In Genesis, God told Adam to name all creatures. How many different kinds of birds can you think of? (Cardinal, blue jay, hummingbird—let each one name some.) Today, there are over 10,000 different species of birds. In the Bible, there are over thirty-seven different references to birds by name.

Noah, his family, and all the animals had been on the ark for many months. The ark had stopped on the top of a mountain. Which bird did Noah choose to send out? (Dove) Each week, Noah would send a dove out to see if there was dry land. Week after week, it would return, and that was a sign it had not been able to find any land. But one day, it returned with an olive branch. Noah grew hopeful. The next week, sending the dove out, it did not return. Noah knew it had found a place to land and make a new home.

The prophet Elijah knew about special birds. Do you remember Elijah, who spoke against King Ahab and his wife Jezebel because they were evil and worshipped idols? The king became so angry that he wanted to kill Elijah, so Elijah ran away and hid. God helped him survive while hiding by sending ravens to feed him.

Isaiah was another prophet. He told the people that they should be like eagles and rise above their problems. Eagles were also mentioned in the book of Ezekiel, when Ezekiel compared himself to one. Another time, Isaiah had a vision of a type of bird. This bird was huge, had six wings, the face of an eagle, and the body of a lion. It was called a seraph.

There is a very special bird mentioned first in the Old Testament, but it later had a place of honor in the New Testament when Jesus was baptized. As Jesus came out of the water, a dove descended from the heavens and rested on Jesus' head. A voice from heaven said, "This is my Son in whom I am well pleased." This illustration showed the people that Jesus was the Son of God.

Jesus spoke many times of sparrows, which are still sold in markets in the Middle Eastern countries. They were very cheap then, two for a penny, but God felt their importance, for He knew when even one of them fell to the ground.

All throughout the Bible, birds, including doves and sparrows, are mentioned. They had importance in the lives of people. Jesus spoke another time of them, when He said, "Look at the birds of the air, they do not sow or reap or store away in barns, and yet your Heavenly Father feeds them" (Matthew 6:26 NIV)

Questions

What bird would you name differently? (Listen to all children.)

What bird helped Elijah? (Raven)

What creature type bird did Isaiah see? (Seraph)

Craft

Make a bird feeder.

Instructions

Cut two small Xs on opposite sides of a twenty-ounce plastic bottle about halfway down from the top. Cut two more Xs near the bottom. Insert wooden spoons. In the bowl area, you may have to open the X more for seeds to spill out. Fill the container with birdseed and replace the top. The birds can obtain seeds from all of the X cuts.

Alternative: cover a pine cone with peanut butter and roll in bird seed. Hang from a tree. This is a good winter feeder.

Supplies

Per child, one twenty-ounce clear plastic bottle, two wooden spoons, bird seed, and funnel. Or pine cones, peanut butter, bird seed, and strings to hang.

If time permits, tell the story about Myrtie the Magpie from the following fable "Why the Magpie's Nest is Unfinished" by Joseph Jacobs.

One day, the Wise Owl called all the birds of the forest together. "It is time that we all learned how to build our nest. First you use your feet and beak."

Myrtie the Magpie, very outspoken, said, "I already have both of those."

The Wise Owl continued, "Use some sticks or twigs."

Myrtie again spoke up. "I know that."

Looking straight at her, he said, "And some of us use mud and straw."

Myrtie was bored and just yawned.

"Many of you have good nests and ideas. Rennie Wren, will you share yours?"

The little wren started the construction of her nest with a nice side opening and a roof for protection. She started telling how she took two reeds and placed them crosswise.

The Warbler and the Oriole demonstrated their nests after Rennie. Myrtie interrupted each one.

Finally, the Owl had enough and said, "Myrtie, if you know it all, then you build your nest and don't forget the roof." Myrtie left the others and went on to build her nest.

Myrtie did not know it all, and to this day, if you find the nest of a magpie, you will be shocked. It is an eyesore. The nest is shapeless with strange looking walls and no roof, and it is very drafty because there is space between the sticks. Maybe Myrtie should have listened.

Foods of the Bible

What kinds of food do you like? Who prepares it? Where do you eat most of the time?

Today, we are going to talk about Bible foods and eat some we can grow or buy today. In Bible times, they didn't have grocery stores like we do but open-air markets. Some of the fruits you might find were pomegranates, figs, dates, apricots, grapes, and maybe some melons. Of course, these all were for sale, so you needed money to purchase them. The vegetables they ate were leeks, onions, garlic, carrots, cucumbers, and lentils, which are like small beans. These vegetables were often cooked in a thick broth, like a soup, and served in flat bowls with bread used as a dipper or spoon. This was the most common food.

Breads were made of wheat and barley, which were harvested in the summer. The grains were ground to remove the husk and turn them into flour for bread. This bread often was flat, like a tortilla or a pancake, because of the way it was cooked. Sometimes, the bakers heated rocks in the fire and the bread was placed on the rock to cook. Barley was the grain often fed to animals because it was cheap. The poorer people bought barley to make their bread.

Meat from cattle was also eaten but mostly on special occasions or to serve to honored guests. Many meats were forbidden by Jewish laws, which are in the books of Leviticus and Deuteronomy. Any animal dying of natural causes could not be eaten, and this included rabbits, camels, pigs, and shellfish. They were forbidden to have meat and milk at the same meal. When an animal was killed, the blood had to be drained before it could be cooked. This made the meat "kosher," that means okay to eat. The Jewish people did not eat pork because they considered it unclean. It's a lot easier to get our meat now, isn't it?

Fish was a staple, meaning a main food. Tilapia from the Sea of Galilee and other kinds of fish were roasted on rocks over a fire, or boiled, or salted and dried so they could be eaten later.

Sheep and goats were milked. They drank some of the milk and used some to make butter and cheese. They had something like cottage cheese that they called curd.

Olives were very important; they were crushed to get the oil out. The oil was used in baking, frying and also in soothing wounds, like the Good Samaritan did.

Grapes were eaten fresh or they were squeezed, and the juice was made into wine, which was the common drink. Wine and water were most often served at meals.

Other fruits were pomegranates, which were also pressed for the juice, and figs. The fig tree was about twenty to thirty feet tall and would produce figs two to three times a year. These were eaten fresh or dried and mixed with honey and made into bread.

The almond tree was used as a symbol that winter was over. They called that tree the "waker" because it was the first to bloom after winter to signify that spring was coming and soon a harvest of nuts.

An evergreen tree called the "carob" had pods that were six to ten inches long. When they were ripe, they contained a sweet syrup that was used to cook with and even make cloth or cosmetics. In the New Testament, these pods were used as animal feed because they were so cheap, but they were also eaten by poor people. In the story of the Prodigal Son, when he fed the hogs their food, which was probably carob pods, he was tempted to eat some.

Questions

Name five foods people of the Bible ate. (Fish, dates, apricots, etc.)

What would you not have eaten? (Let each child name something.)

Who cooked the foods? (Usually the mother or the servants)

Activity

Make bread to be eaten with a Bible meal.

Instructions

Prior to class, make lentil soup (recipe included) or purchase cans of bean or thick vegetable soup. Prepare the dough for the flat bread and give each child a ball. Demonstrate how to flatten it by hand and cook on a griddle. Caution the children about getting burned.

Serve the food in wooden salad bowls, no spoons, only bread to dip and eat while sitting on the floor. Have water to drink. Also serve a plate of olives, figs, dates, or grapes or any other Bible food.

Supplies

Soup, flat bread ingredients, bowl for mixing bread, wooden bowls, water, plate of fruits or other Bible foods. Enjoy this meal. Children may not like the lentil soup, but encourage them to taste it.

Recipe for Flat Bread

2 cups flour

3/4 cup water

1/2 tsp. salt

Olive oil to coat griddle

Mix first three ingredients and form into a ball. Knead until smooth.

Make small balls of dough to be rolled or patted thin for frying.

Spread olive oil on griddle and place flat dough. Cook on both sides.

This is a tough bread; this recipe will make about eleven small circles. They can also be dipped in honey.

Recipe for Lentil Soup

1 onion chopped

1 bay leaf

1/4 cup olive oil

1 (14.5 oz.) can tomatoes

2 carrots, diced

2 cups dried lentils

2 cloves garlic minced

8 cups water

1 tsp. dried oregano

2 tbs. vinegar

1 tsp. dried basil

Salt and pepper to taste

In a large soup pot, heat oil over medium heat.

Add onions, carrots, and celery; cook and stir until onion is tender.

Stir in garlic, bay leaf, oregano, and basil; cook for two minutes.

Stir in lentils and add water and tomatoes. Bring to a boil. Reduce heat and simmer for at least one hour. If soup is too thick, add more water.

When ready to serve, stir in vinegar and season to taste with salt and pepper and more vinegar if desired. As in Bible times, use bread instead of a spoon with this soup.

New Testament

A Blessing from God

Luke 1:5–25, 1:57–80

During the reign of King Herod, many Jewish priests served in the temple in Jerusalem. One priest, Zechariah, and his wife, Elizabeth, were descendants of Aaron. Do you remember Aaron? He was the brother who helped Moses lead the Israelites out of Egypt to the Promised Land.

Zechariah and Elizabeth were very devoted to God, and they carefully obeyed all His laws. They had never been blessed with children and had grown very old. The time had come for Zechariah to serve in the temple. He was chosen to enter the most holy place in the temple and keep the incense burning on the altar. As he was preparing the incense, an angel appeared to him. He was afraid.

"Don't be afraid, Zechariah," the angel said. "The Lord has heard your prayers. Elizabeth will have a son, and you will name him John. He will be a great man of rugged character and will prepare the way for the Messiah."

Zechariah was shocked. How could that happen? He told the angel he and his wife were old.

The angel replied, "I am Gabriel! I stand in the very presence of God. He sent me with this good news. And now, because you haven't believed, you will be silent; unable to speak until the child is born, for all this will come true." The angel disappeared.

Zechariah was still in shock when he finally came out of the temple. Because of his age, the people thought something had happened to him. When he tried to talk and tell them about Gabriel, they could hear no words. When he used gestures to try to let them know what had happened, they realized he must have seen a vision.

Everything happened just as Gabriel had said. Soon, Elizabeth was going to have a baby. Before Elizabeth's child was born, her niece Mary visited her. Mary had also had seen the angel Gabriel. Gabriel told Mary that she too would have a son and to name him Jesus. He would be the long-awaited Messiah for the people.

When it came time, a beautiful son was born to Elizabeth and Zechariah. Eight days after the birth, according to their custom, they took the baby to the temple to officially name him. The priest asked Elizabeth the baby's name and expected her to say "Zechariah," because that was his father's name, but instead, she said, "John."

The priest knew of no one in the family of Zechariah named John, so he asked Zechariah about the name. Zechariah used a slate to answer because he still could not speak. He wrote the name "John." Right then, Zechariah realized he could talk again, and he started praising God. He told the priests and the people that a Savior would be sent from the line of David just as prophesized many years before. He said that his precious son, John, would prepare the way for this Savior.

John was brought up to love, worship, and be faithful to God just as Zechariah and Elizabeth had done all their lives.

Questions

Who was Zechariah? (A priest and the father of John)

Who came to visit Elizabeth? (Her niece Mary)

What was the name of Zechariah's son? (John)

Craft

Paint angel votive candles.

Instructions

Prior to class, draw an angel shape on each votive holder with a permanent marker. Instruct the children to paint the figure with gold or white and paint the rest of the glass with any color they choose. Suggest painting with many colors to make it look like stained glass.

Place a candle in each glass for them to take home and light. Tell them that as the candle is burning, they should tell their parents this story.

Supplies

Votive glass holders and candles, one per child, acrylic or glass paint.

Another Miracle

Matthew 1:18–24; Luke 1:26–38, 2:1–20

Remember the story about Elizabeth and Zechariah? This story is also about another miracle that was going to happen. A young girl named Mary was about to be visited by Gabriel, an angel from God.

When Gabriel greeted Mary, she was scared. He told her not to be afraid because God was with her and she was going to have a baby. His name would be Jesus. Mary questioned how that could happen because she wasn't married. Gabriel said that this child would have the Holy Spirit as his father. He told her that Elizabeth, her aunt, was also going to have a baby even though Elizabeth was old. "Nothing is impossible with God."

Mary was honored, but she was still scared. She left her home and went to visit Elizabeth. When Mary walked in, Elizabeth immediately knew that Mary had been blessed, and she greeted her warmly. Mary stayed with Elizabeth until it was time for Elizabeth's son, John, to be born. Returning to Nazareth, Mary told Joseph, the man she was engaged to, that she was going to have a baby. After hearing the news, Joseph wanted to send her away privately. He felt she had disgraced him with someone else. He would break their engagement.

But that night, he had a dream that changed his mind. He too was visited by an angel. The angel told him, "Don't be afraid to take Mary as your wife, for she will give birth to a son, and you are to give him the name Jesus, because he will save his people from sin." Joseph knew the prophesies of old had predicted that one day a Savior for God's people was to come, but he never thought he would be part of that plan. He decided to still take Mary as his wife, and she would have a son named Jesus, who would become this Savior.

Joseph and Mary were married and lived as a couple. When it came closer for her to give birth, Caesar, who was the Roman emperor, would change the birthplace of Jesus. This too was following the prophesy in the Old Testament. Herod was appointed by Caesar to help control the Jewish people. Knowing that Caesar needed a census telling the exact number of Jews there were, Herod forced all Jews to journey to their birthplaces to register and be counted for taxes.

Joseph was from the line of David, so he and Mary headed to Bethlehem. He knew the trip would be hard on Mary, but they had no choice. He knew God would be with them all the time.

The journey to Bethlehem was indeed hard for Mary, and she soon needed to rest. Joseph knew the time for the birth was near. After finding no place in an inn, like a motel, Joseph was finally told of a stable where they could stay. A stable is where animals were kept and fed and it would be dry, warm, and safe.

That night, Mary gave birth to the most precious baby boy. As she and Joseph looked at the baby, Mary whispered, "And his name will be called Jesus." Everything said by the prophet Isaiah in the Old Testament was coming true. Mary wrapped her baby in swaddling clothes and laid him in a manger, which was a feeding box for the animals. Do you know what swaddling clothes were? They were strips of material a mother would wrap tightly around the baby to keep him warm and feel secure. They also served as diapers so that she could change them.

The night Jesus was born, God was still working. In the fields near Bethlehem, a group of men called shepherds were tending their sheep. The angel appeared to them and said, "Fear not. For, behold, I bring you good tiding of great joy, which shall be to all people. For unto you is born this day in the city of David, a Savior, which is Christ the Lord." The whole heavens were filled with angels singing, "Glory to God in the highest, and on earth peace, and goodwill toward men."

As the shepherds started toward Bethlehem to see this Savior, they were very excited. When they found Mary and Joseph, they told them what they had seen on the hillside. These shepherds were the first visitors for baby Jesus.

Three wise men, who had followed a certain star, also came to visit Jesus. The gifts they brought helped Joseph provide for his family. God's plan was working. This baby was born in Bethlehem, was named Jesus, and would be a Savior to all.

Questions

What did Gabriel tell Mary to name her son? (Jesus)

Why did Mary and Joseph go to Bethlehem? (To be counted for taxes)

Who were the first visitors to see Jesus? (The shepherds)

Craft

Make a "Fear Not" bracelet to remind the children of the angel's words.

Instructions

Each child threads colored beads of choice on the cord with glow-in-the-dark beads spelling "Fear Not" at the center. When they have enough to go around their wrist, tie, knot, and secure with glue. The glow-in-the-dark beads will glow after exposed to light.

Supplies

Regular colorful "Pony" beads, letter beads spelling "Fear Not," and elastic cording.

Jesus as a Boy

Luke 2:41–51

After Jesus was born in Bethlehem, he spent the next year or two in Egypt. When Jesus was a child, he probably acted a lot like children today. The Bible says, "And the child grew and became strong; he was filled with wisdom, and the grace of God was upon Him" (Luke 2:40 NIV).

Mary and Joseph moved from Egypt to Nazareth, where Jesus grew up. He was the oldest child of several, perhaps seven brothers and sisters. According to Jewish custom, the boys would be taught all the laws and rules for their people in the schools of the synagogues. The girls of the families were taught at home by mothers and grandmothers.

The books of Exodus and Deuteronomy in the Bible tell of the three specific holidays, Passover, Pentecost, and Tabernacles, that the Jewish people celebrated. All Jewish males had to travel to the temple in Jerusalem for these holidays, but distance often prevented them from attending all three. Passover was the one most attended. All members of the families would travel, but only the males and young boys, age twelve and above, would be able to participate in the service.

When it was time to celebrate Passover, Jesus traveled to Jerusalem with His parents and other family and friends. Jesus must have been excited about the trip. That was the first year he would be permitted to go into the temple with Joseph.

When the festival was over, the caravan of families departed Jerusalem and headed home to Nazareth. They had traveled all day. As night approached, Mary and Joseph realized that Jesus was not with them. They had not missed Him during the day because they thought He was just walking with friends, but He was missing. They were afraid and thought Jesus must have also felt fear being away from them. Can you imagine these feelings they had? Have you ever been lost from your parents?

They rushed back to Jerusalem and frantically searched everywhere and finally found Him in the temple. He was talking with the teachers and rabbis. Jesus was so involved in conversation with them that He didn't even act as if He had missed his parents. His parents were concerned, but it appeared that Jesus was not. It had been three days since they had seen Him. He was listening to the teachers, asking questions, and as the Bible says, "Everyone who heard Him speak about the scriptures was amazed" (Luke 2:47 NIV). How could a boy only twelve years old have so much knowledge of the Scriptures and God?

Turning to Jesus, Mary asked why He was still there and told Him they had been so worried. Jesus replied, "Why were you searching for me? Didn't you know I would be in my Father's house?" This is the only record of conversation between Jesus and His parents, but He left with them and headed back to Nazareth. Jesus knew he had a special relationship with God, but Mary and Joseph were his parents, and He would be obedient to them.

Little is known about what Jesus did for the next eighteen years. He grew as any other boy. He learned the trade of Joseph, which was carpentry, and He took his place in the Jewish community. He grew just as all other Jewish boys and learned the Scriptures and laws for living.

Questions

What holidays did the Jewish people celebrate? (Passover, Pentecost, and Tabernacles)

Why did Jesus stay in Jerusalem? (To talk to rabbis and priests)

How old was Jesus at that time? (Twelve)

Craft or Activity

Just like children do today, the children of Bible times played with what they had— sand to build roads and pieces of wood, for instance, and they had foot races and played stick ball. Jesus referred to children many times in His teachings as an adult, so He knew children liked to play.

Instructions

For stick ball, divide the children into two teams. Give each person a small stick to hit the ball. Have a goal set up for each team. This can be set up like soccer today. Scoring is by hitting the ball into their team's goal.

The ball in Bible times may have been woven of cloth or vines and the sticks any found from the carpentry shop or trees.

Supplies

Sticks or pieces of wood, a ball, and energy.

Calling of the Disciples

Luke 5–6

Jesus was about thirty when He began His ministry of teaching and healing. Crowds gathered everywhere He went. One day, when He was near the Sea of Galilee, crowds were pressing closer because they wanted to hear Him. Jesus got into a boat owned by Simon Peter and Andrew, who were brothers. Jesus asked them to row Him out into the lake so He could preach to the crowds. Simon Peter and Andrew obeyed and took Him farther out into the lake and listened as Jesus spoke.

After He finished speaking, Jesus told Peter to go out to a deeper area and put down their nets. Peter said they had fished all night and had caught nothing, but he would obey Jesus. Soon, the nets were so full of fish that they began to tear. They called to their partners, James and John, for help. The boats were so full of fish that they were afraid they would sink. They had never caught so many fish. Peter realized the power of Jesus and felt unworthy to be near Him. Jesus looked at Peter and said, "Follow me and I will make you fishers of men!"

As soon as they got back to shore, Peter, Andrew, James, and John left their boats and followed Jesus. Later, Matthew, a tax collector, was also called to follow. These five were among the crowds that went with Jesus everywhere, listening to His teaching and watching Him heal the sick and lame. Soon, even more people started following Him everywhere.

Jesus knew that He needed to select a smaller group to become His close disciples, His inner circle of followers. Going alone to the mountainside, He prayed all night. The next morning, Jesus chose twelve men to become His disciples: Simon, whom He called Peter; Andrew, the brother of Peter; James and John, the sons of Zebedee; Phillip; Bartholomew; Matthew; Thomas; Simon the Zealot; Judas, the son of James; and Judas Iscariot. Among them were fishermen, a tax collector, a zealot who belonged to a political group against rulers, a betrayer, and others who were good, faithful men. All were different in actions and talents. Jesus would be with these twelve men for three years. They would love and follow Him throughout His ministry.

(Discuss with the children different people of the local congregation. All cannot be preachers, song leaders, or teachers. Some are lawyers, doctors, businesspeople, cashiers at Walmart, etc. Point out that Jesus calls everyone to follow Him, and He called the very common people such as fishermen first. God has a place for everyone.)

Questions

How many disciples did Jesus choose? (Twelve)

Who was called first? (Peter and Andrew)

What did Jesus tell the fishermen? ("Follow me and I will make you fishers of men.")

Craft

Make a swivel bracelet or anklet. Explain that a swivel is what fishermen use to connect the fishing line to the hook.

Instructions

Give each child about ten swivels according to wrist or ankle size. Open and connect them to form a chain, and then connect those at the ends to form a bracelet. Tell them that wearing their bracelets will remind them they are connected to Jesus. He said, "Follow me and I will make you fishers of men."

Duplicate the text of the handout card, one per student. The bracelet and card message are good ways for them to remember the story of how the disciples were chosen.

Supplies

Swivels and handout cards. Swivels can be purchased in the fishing section of a Walmart or a sports store.

Handout Card Text

As the swivel connects the line to the Hook,
so are you the connector between God and man.

In Matthew 4:19, Jesus says, "Follow Me
and I will make you Fishers of Men."

A Wedding

John 2

Jesus, His mother Mary, and a few disciples were among the guests at a big wedding in Cana. When Jesus entered the home, He noticed several large water vessels near the entrance. These jugs held around twenty-seven gallons of water that was used mainly for washing feet. It was customary to have water for such foot washing because people wore sandals and the roads were dusty. Servants usually washed the feet of those coming into a house.

Jesus and His disciples were enjoying the festivities. Mary approached Jesus and said, "The wine has run out, and there is nothing to drink." Mary was a friend of the family, so that was a big concern. Jesus replied, "Why are you telling me this? It is not my responsibility nor my time for miracles."

Mary didn't listen. Pointing to Jesus, she told the servants just to do whatever He told them to do. When the servants came to Jesus and told Him what His mother had said, Jesus told them to go to the water jugs near the entrance, dip some water out, and take it to the banquet master to taste. That person was the one who had planned and prepared all the food and drink. He had to approve of everything that was served. He tasted the water, which Jesus had turned into delicious wine, and told the bridegroom that normally, people served the best wine first and cheaper wine after that, but this time it was the opposite—the best had been served last. The banquet master was shocked and pleased.

The disciples of Jesus had heard and seen the foot washing water being turned into wine. They realized He was special and wanted to follow Jesus wherever He went. This was the first miracle of Jesus.

Questions

Why were Jesus, Mary, and the disciples in Cana? (For a wedding)

What were the water jugs near the entrance for? (Feet washing)

How many miracles had Jesus performed before this wedding? (None)

Activity

Enjoy a wedding feast with "wine." Have an abundant amount of food as would be served at a great party.

Instructions

Have mothers prepare sandwiches, cookies, and other "wedding" food to be served on dainty plates. Let a child prepare the "wine". Prior to the meeting, add a package of grape drink mix as Kool-Aid to a colored pitcher. Have the children add clear water to the pitcher and stir. The water will turn to "wine". Good visual demonstration.

Supplies

Grape Kool-Aid, colored pitcher, water, dainty plates, napkins, and wedding treats.

John Baptizes Jesus

Matthew 3:1–17; Mark 1:9–11; Luke 3:1–3; John 1:32–34

"In the wilderness prepare the way for the Lord, make straight in the wilderness a highway for our God" (Isaiah 40:3 NIV). This Scripture was coming true. A strange man named John who lived in the desert was prophesizing the coming of the Messiah. He was speaking about Jesus. John was the fulfillment of the promises of Isaiah that the world would see a Messiah.

John was born the son of Zechariah and Elizabeth. At the time of his birth, both parents were old and would probably not live to see their son begin his ministry. John grew up in the desert, and as the Bible says, looked rugged and wild. He made his clothes of skins and ate locusts and wild honey. After hearing him talk, many people thought he was the prophet Elijah returning. John had a purpose and mission. He was to prepare the way for the ministry of Jesus.

When preaching to people, John always said, "Repent, turn from your evil ways, and ask God for forgiveness." The people who believed what he said wanted John to baptize them as a sign they were repenting of their sins. That is why he was called John the Baptist.

John was preaching in the country, but when Jesus started His ministry, He stayed near the cities. Their teachings were often compared, and many asked John if he was the expected Messiah or Savior. John told them he would never be as great as the Messiah. He even said, "After me will come one more powerful than I, the thongs of whose sandals I am not worthy to stoop down and untie" (Mark 1:7 NIV). John would also say that he baptized with water but that God would send someone to baptize with the Holy Spirit.

The paths of Jesus and John crossed many times, and John would point Jesus out to the people around. Both had disciples and followers. Two of John's followers would later be among the closest disciples of Jesus. John never said he was the "savior" of the people but only the one to prepare the way for the Savior.

John was baptizing many people in the Jordan River when Jesus came to him. John recognized Jesus and said, "Jesus, I need to be baptized by you." John felt unworthy because he recognized Jesus as the Messiah and Son of God. John was just a man, but he baptized Jesus. As Jesus came up out of the water, the Holy Spirit in the shape of a dove descended on Jesus' head, and a voice from heaven was heard, "This is my Son, whom I love, with Him I am well pleased" (Matthew 3:17 NIV). This baptism showed the people that Jesus was the expected Savior and the Son of God.

John continued his preaching. He told only the truth and did not matter who it concerned. His death came later, when he talked against King Herod and his wife. Because of her trickery, John the Baptist was killed.

Questions

Was John the expected Messiah? (No, Jesus was.)

Did John have disciples? (Yes)

Why John was called "John the Baptist"? (He baptized people.)

Craft

Make a collage of the life of John.

Instructions

Draw pictures or cut some out of magazines that signify the life of John the Baptist and paste them on construction paper or card stock. Suggestions for pictures: locusts, sandals, beards, long hair, sand of the desert, a dove, honey, leather, or anything that reminds them of the character they see as John. Overlap the pictures and seal with Mod Podge sealant.

Supplies

Magazines, markers, construction paper, scissors, glue, and sealant.

Optional

Color the picture of Jesus being baptized.

"**This is my Son, whom I love;
with Him I am well pleased.**"

Jesus Spoke and the People Listened

Matthew 5–6

When Jesus spoke to the people, He used words they could easily understand. The Pharisees, the rulers of the temple, had interpreted the laws of God and had given strict rules how to obey them. There were so many laws that it was becoming impossible to obey all of them. Jesus told the people that God's kingdom was for everyone, not for just a chosen few as the Pharisees taught. He showed people how to love and care for each other. When Jesus spoke of the coming of God's kingdom, He didn't mean that there would be political rulers, even though some people were expecting a new government. He meant that God would rule over the hearts of people and their lives would be changed.

Prophets of the Old Testament told of a Messiah, a Savior for the world. The more Jesus spoke and the more miracles He performed, the people began to feel that earlier prophesies had finally come true, and Jesus was the long-expected Messiah and Savior. They would follow Him everywhere to watch and learn. Of course, not everyone liked Him. He angered the Sanhedrin, the Jewish rulers, because He was becoming so popular.

The stories Jesus used were called parables and always concerned something the people could understand. He often spoke of salt, lamps, light, money, planting crops, and caring for animals, which were the normal surroundings and activities of people everywhere.

Sitting on the side of a hill, Jesus talked about the blessings all people had. Each time He spoke, He started with "Blessed are," wanting them to understand they were truly blessed. These are called the "Beatitudes" and are in Matthew 5:3–10. They are reminders that everyone is blessed and can be happy.

Another teaching of Jesus was concerning prayer. Jesus told the people that when they prayed, they were praying to God, not man. He told the story of a person who wanted everyone to see how righteous he was and would often pray on a street corner where there was a big crowd. His prayers were elaborate—he used lots of big, flowery words to draw attention to himself. He wanted everyone to think he was special and very religious and to hear him pray. Jesus told the people that when they prayed, they should speak to God and not to people. His example of the perfect prayer is one that is used in many churches every Sunday morning as part of their service. It is called the Lord's Prayer and is in Matthew 6:9–13.

He also taught people how to live with each other. Jesus said, "Do unto others as you would have them do unto you." This is called the Golden Rule, and it is in Matthew 7:12. Jesus said we should treat people like we want to be treated, not the way they often treat us.

Jesus taught and lived among the people for three years on earth. The disciples listened and learned from His teachings, and so did all the people who constantly surrounded Him. However, there were certain groups, the Sadducees and Pharisees that did not like all the attention Jesus received and would try to catch Him in not obeying all the Jewish laws.

Questions

Where are the Beatitudes found? (Matthew 5:3–10)

Where is the Lord's Prayer found? (Matthew 6:9–13)

What is the Golden Rule? (Do unto others as you would have them do unto you: Matthew 7:12)

Craft or Activity

Using bland food, a candle, and a ruler, explain some of the teachings of Jesus.

Instructions

Taste bland food such as mashed potatoes or rice with no salt or seasoning. Then taste it after adding salt.

Light a dark room with a candle or flashlight. Talk about entering a dark room, especially at night, and turning on the light. Illustrate a lamp without a shade versus one with a shade. This illustrates the story of the light under a bushel basket.

Prior to class, purchase or write the Golden Rule on a ruler to be given to each child. Bookmarks written with the Lord's Prayer and the Beatitudes can also be purchased.

Supplies

Bland food, salt, candles, matches, rulers, or bookmarks.

Optional

In the room, display a picture of Jesus in the center and copies of the Beatitudes, the Lord's Prayer, and the Golden Rule beneath the picture. Each week, important Scriptures can be added, and they can be memorized. Sample Scriptures are from the King James Version, but another version that children can more easily understand can be used.

Scriptures to Memorize: King James Version

For God so loved the world that He gave His only begotten Son, that whosoever believeth in him should not perish, but have everlasting life. (John 3:16)

I can do all things through Christ which strengthened me. (Philippians 4:13)

Be strong and of a good courage, be not afraid, neither be thou dismayed: for the Lord thy God is with thee whither thou goest. (Joshua 1:8)

God is our refuge and strength, a very present help in trouble. (Psalms 46:1)

Thy word is a lamp unto my feet and a light unto my path. (Psalms 119:105)

Children obey your parents in all things for this is well pleasing to the Lord. (Colossians 3:20)

And be ye kind one to another, tenderhearted, forgiving one another, even as God for Christ's sake hath forgiven you. (Ephesians 4:32)

But God commendeth his love toward us, in that while we were still sinners, Christ died for us. (Romans 5:8)

Jesus said to them, I am the way the truth, and the life, no man cometh unto the Father, but by Me. (John 14:6)

Whatsoever ye shall ask in prayer, believing, ye shall receive. (Matthew 21:22)

Be ye doers of the word, and not hearers only. (James 1:22)

For the wages of sin is death; but the gift of God is eternal life though Jesus Christ our Lord. (Romans: 6:23)

Rejoice in the Lord always; and again I say, Rejoice. (Philippians 4:4)

For where your treasure is, there will your heart be also. (Luke 12:34)

In the beginning God created heavens and earth. (Genesis 1:1)

Study to shew thyself approved unto God, a workman that needeth not to be ashamed, rightly dividing the word of truth. (2 Timothy 2:15)

The Lord's Prayer

Our Father, who art in heaven,
Hallowed by thy Name.
Thy kingdom come.
Thy will be done,
On earth as it is in heaven.
Give us this day our daily bread.
And forgive us our trespasses,
As we forgive those
Who trespass against us.
And lead us not into temptation,
But deliver us from evil.
For thine is the kingdom,
And the power, and the glory,
For ever and ever.
Amen.

Golden Rule

Do unto others
As you would have them do unto you.
(Matthew 7:12)

The Eight Beatitudes of Jesus

Blessed are the poor in spirit,
for theirs is the kingdom of heaven.

Blessed are they who mourn,
for they shall be comforted.

Blessed are the meek,
for they shall inherit the earth.

Blessed are they who hunger and thirst for righteousness,
for they shall be satisfied.

Blessed are the merciful,
for they shall obtain mercy.

Blessed are the pure of heart,
for they shall see God.

Blessed are the peacemakers,
for they shall be called children of God.

Blessed are they who are persecuted for the sake of righteousness,
for theirs is the kingdom of heaven.
(Matthew 5:3-10)

Give Them Something to Eat

Mark 6:30–44, 8:1–9

The gospels of Matthew, Mark, Luke, and John are filled with the life and teachings of Jesus. Jesus began His ministry about the age of thirty, and He was becoming so popular that a crowd of people would follow Him everywhere. When Jesus taught, He used stories the people could understand and illustrated them by talking about common things such as planting crops, birds, oil for lamps, and something as small as a mustard seed. These stories were called parables, and there are many of them in the Bible.

One day, Jesus had been teaching on a hillside, a good place for all the people to hear Him. Toward the end of the day, the disciples began to worry. They knew that soon these people would be hungry, and they were far away from any market. They told Jesus to send some people away to buy food. Jesus immediately answered them, "You feed them." The disciples knew that wasn't possible because it would take more money than they had to buy enough food to feed them.

Jesus told them to check with people in the crowd to find out if anyone had brought anything to eat. They found a boy who had come to hear Jesus; and his mother had packed him a lunch of two fish and five small loaves of bread. When they brought it to Jesus, He took the food, raised it to the heavens, and asked the Lord's blessing on it. He gave it to the disciples to distribute among the people. After telling all the people to sit down, the disciples passed out the fish and loaves. Everyone had enough to eat, and when the disciples picked up the remaining food, they were amazed, for there was enough left to fill twelve baskets.

This was another example of the abundant blessings God gives us. Not only had over five thousand been fed, but also, the disciples and the people there had witnessed another miracle from Jesus.

Another time, Jesus was teaching the crowds and had compassion on them when it came time to eat. Many had been with Him over three days, and Jesus didn't want to send them away. He said to the disciples, "Feed them." Just like before, the disciples answered that they were too far from anyplace where they could buy food even if they had the money. They should never have asked Jesus how He was going to supply it. Jesus looked at them and asked what they had. They answered about the same as before, but that time, they found seven small loaves of bread and a few small fish. Remember, dried fish and bread were common food for the people. Again, Jesus asked for the Lord's blessing, and all were able to eat. There were seven baskets of broken pieces left after feeding four thousand people. Jesus never let any of His followers go hungry.

Questions

Why were there so many people following Jesus? (They wanted to hear Him teach.)
How many times did Jesus feed the crowds? (At least twice)
How much food was left over? (First time, twelve baskets; second time, seven)

Craft

Make a fish and bread mobile.

Instructions

Using fish and bread templates, cut two identical sides for each. Have children make two fish and five loaves for each mobile. Glue sides together, leaving holes at the bottom for stuffing. Decorate with crayons, paint, tissue paper, etc. Stuff with tissue paper and glue or staple closed. Punch a hole near the top center of each for hanging. Cut yarn in varying lengths and insert one through each hole. Secure and tie the other end to the hanger.

Supplies

Fish and bread template, construction paper, crayons or paint, stickers, and one wire clothes hanger per child.

Optional

Color the picture of Jesus asking God's blessings.

Walking on Water

Matthew 14:22–33; John 6:16–24

Have you ever been swimming in a lake or the ocean? Is there any way you can step on water and not sink to the bottom? Jesus could, but we all know He could do a lot of things we can't.

The day had been special; over five thousand people had experienced a miracle when the disciples distributed food from only five small loaves of bread and two fish. Jesus had sent His disciples ahead of Him so He could go to the mountainside to pray and be alone with God. All the disciples boarded a boat to take them to the other shore. Early that morning, the winds and water got higher. Several of the disciples were experienced in handling a boat, so at first they were not concerned. They had rowed to the middle of the lake, about three miles from shore, and they started having trouble keeping the boat from sinking. All of a sudden, they saw someone walking toward them. How could that be? They were not close to shore. They said, "It's a ghost!" and grew more frightened. It was Jesus, but they didn't recognize Him. There is no way He could be walking on the water.

Jesus said, "It is I, don't be afraid." Peter said, "If it is really you, then tell me to come to you on the water." Jesus reached out his hand and said, "Come." All Peter could think about was going to his Master and immediately got out of the boat. He was not even thinking about being in the middle of the lake. Peter was walking on the water when suddenly he realized where he was. He saw the waves and felt the wind, and he took his eyes off Jesus. That was when he started to sink.

"Lord, save me!" Peter cried.

Jesus reached out to him and said, "You of little faith, why did you doubt?" Peter realized that as long as he kept his eyes on Jesus, everything was fine, but when he looked at his surroundings, he started to sink. After the disciples pulled Peter and Jesus into the boat, they worshipped Jesus, saying, "Truly you are the Son of God." This was the first time the disciples used that title to address Jesus. The lesson that Jesus taught the disciples that day was that they should keep their eyes and prayers on Him always.

Questions

Why wasn't Jesus with the disciples? (They went in the boat, but He needed to be alone to pray.)

How far where they from the shore? (About three miles, in the middle of the lake.)

Did they see a ghost? (No, they saw Jesus.)

Craft

Are you a floater or a sinker?

Instructions

Collect a large bowl of water and many objects such as Ivory soap, Dial soap, spoon, foil ball, wood, coins, egg, etc. Choose several that will float or sink. Let children take turns demonstrating.

Snack

Blue Jell-O or make Jell-O Jigglers in individual cups with gummy candies on toothpicks to represent Jesus and Peter.

Supplies

Jell-O, gummy candies, floating and sinking objects, bowl of water, and paper towels for cleanup.

Optional

Color the picture of Jesus walking on water.

Recipe for Jell-O Jigglers

1 1/2 cups boiling water

2 (6 ounce) packages of gelatin (blue)

Dissolve gelatin in water. Pour into cups and place in refrigerator to gel.

Double recipe as needed for the number of children.

Woman at the Well

John 4

As Jesus and His disciples traveled through Samaria, they neared the town of Sychar. This was the area of Jacob's well dating back to the Old Testament times. Because most of the Holy Land is very dry, wells were important to the people, livestock, and crops. The disciples had gone into the town of Sychar, but Jesus chose to rest near this well.

It was the job of the women to get water for their families. When a Samaritan woman came for water, Jesus asked her for a drink. The woman recognized Jesus as a Jew and said, "You are a Jew, and I am a Samaritan woman. How can you ask me for a drink?" The Jews despised the Samaritans, and drinking from a cup handled by a Samaritan was considered unclean. Also, Jewish men would never speak to a Samaritan woman, but this did not stop Jesus.

Jesus told her He could give her "living water," meaning the grace of God for eternal life. She said she saw no way for Him to get that water from the deep well. Jesus said, "Anyone who drinks this water will become thirsty, but with the water I give, they will never thirst." The woman answered, "Sir, give me that water so I won't have to come every day and draw water."

Jesus told her to go home and return with her husband. She told Him she had no husband. Jesus knew the man she was living with at that time was not her husband, and He told her that He knew that she had been married five times. She thought Jesus must have been a prophet to know all about her life. She told Him that her people knew the Messiah was coming. She said that when He came, everything concerning prophesies would be explained. Jesus said, "I who speak to you am He."

When the disciples returned with the food, they were shocked to find Jesus talking to a Samaritan woman. No one asked the woman what she wanted or "Jesus, why are you talking with her?" They knew that Jewish religious men almost never spoke to women. The woman left her water jug and went back to town. She told everyone to come with her because she had met a Jewish man who knew all about her life. She felt that this man must be the Messiah they had been waiting for.

Many of the people came back with her to see Jesus. They believed in Him because of the woman's testimony. They invited Him to stay so they could also hear His words. Jesus and the disciples stayed two days. During that time, many who heard Him believed that Jesus was the long-awaited Messiah. He had come for all people, including the Samaritans.

Questions

Where were the disciples? (Buying food)

Who came to the well? (A Samaritan woman)

Did she tell others about Jesus? (Yes, everyone she saw)

Craft

Make a desktop well.

Instructions

Prior to the class, attach masking tape around the sharp edges of a clean soup or vegetable can, one per child. Instruct the children they will make a well similar to the one Jesus and the woman were near. They should attach small pebbles or rocks around the outside of the can using either hot glue or a cooler melting point glue, or a glue like Aleene's Tacky. Caution the children about using hot glue.

The glue and stones need to be completely dry before taking home. This finished "well" can be used to hold pens or pencils.

Supplies

One empty can per child, small stones or pebbles, and glue gun or other types of glue, and masking tape.

Optional

Color the picture of the woman at the well.

Healing on the Sabbath

John 5

The reputation of Jesus had spread from town to town. Many had witnessed miracles being performed from the feeding of thousands to the healing of diseases. Crowds followed Him everywhere, especially those with health problems for they wanted to be healed.

On the Sabbath, Sunday, Jesus and His disciples entered Jerusalem. The Sabbath was a holy day, and since the beginning, when God created the world, it was set aside as a day of rest. The laws of the Jewish people didn't allow for anyone to work on the Sabbath, and the Pharisees and Sadducees, rulers of the Jews, were ready to enforce these rules.

Near the gate going into Jerusalem was a pool called Bethsaida. This pool was thought to have healing powers, especially when the water was stirred. Disabled, lame, blind, and paralyzed people would gather around the pool in hopes of being healed.

Jesus saw a man on a mat. He had been paralyzed for thirty-eight years. Each day, he was brought there in hopes of being healed. Jesus came to him and asked, "Do you want to get well?" The man answered, "Sir, I have no one to help me into the pool when the water is stirred. While I am trying to get in, someone else goes down ahead of me." The first one into the water would be healed. This man didn't know Jesus was a healer because he thought the pool was the only healer.

Jesus said, "Get up, pick up your mat and walk." The man got up, rolled up his mat, and started walking. He was so excited that he may have started running as he headed home. The excitement for him was so great that he didn't even see Jesus walk quietly away among the crowds.

On the way home, he was stopped by the Jewish rulers. They said, "It is the Sabbath, and the law forbids you to work." They considered carrying his mat working. He told them that a man had healed him and told him to get up and walk. He didn't even think about it being the Sabbath for he had not walked for over thirty years. He was healed, and that was all that mattered to him. The rulers asked him about the person who had healed him. He could not tell them it was Jesus because he didn't know.

Later, while worshipping in the temple and rejoicing for being healed, the man was again visited by Jesus. Jesus told him that since he was healed, he should go and sin no more. When Jesus lived, people thought that illnesses were caused by someone sinning. The man now realized that he had been healed by Jesus, and Jesus was the healer everyone had been talking about. The man immediately sought out the rulers and pointed to Jesus as the one who had healed him.

The rulers scolded Jesus for healing on the Sabbath. Jesus replied, "My Father is always at work this very day and I too am working." The rulers felt Jesus had committed two sins—working on the Sabbath and calling God His father. They were going to try even harder to get rid of Jesus, for He was becoming too popular with the people. They felt that more would follow Jesus and His rules instead of the Jewish law and not listen to them.

Questions

What day did Jesus heal the man? (Sabbath)

What did Jesus ask the paralyzed man? (Do you want to be healed?)

What did Jesus tell him? (Take up your mat and walk.)

Craft

Weave a mat using either fabric or construction paper.

Instructions

Prior to meeting, cut twenty one-inch strips ten inches long from two different colors of a heavy fabric or construction paper per child. Using one color, lay their strips vertically (up and down) side by side. With the other strips, start in the middle, and weave horizontally (across) "over and under" pattern through all the vertical strips. Continue weaving, alternating next row "under-over" pattern. They will have to move them closer together as they weave. When completed, fold edges under and glue. This is small, but the same way the mat of the lame man was woven so it could be folded or rolled up and carried. This technique was also used for sleeping mats.

Supplies

Fabric or construction paper cut in horizontal and vertical strips per child, and glue. Younger groups do better with paper, and they may need help.

Optional

Color or paint the picture of Jesus and the healed man.

Jesus Speaks and the Waters Listen

Matthew 8:23–27; Mark 4:36–41; Luke 8:22–25

Jesus and His disciples had walked several miles. He had been teaching and healing the crowds all day, and they had followed Him everywhere.

Coming to the Sea of Galilee, Jesus and the disciples boarded a boat to cross to the other side and get away from the crowds for a while. The Sea of Galilee is in a valley surrounded by mountains. Winds can come up fast, making water travel dangerous. His disciples who were fishermen were used to the sudden changes of the winds, so all in the boat felt safe.

Jesus, being very tired, soon fell asleep on a cushion in the front of the boat. The water was calm, the air cool, and the night good. Everything suddenly changed; a storm came up. The waves grew higher, water was splashing over the sides of their boat, and they were afraid it would sink. The boat was being tossed about furiously by the waves, and nothing they did helped. Becoming more afraid, they woke Jesus up, saying, "Teacher, look at this storm. Don't you care if we drown?"

Turning toward the wind and waves, He said, "Quiet. Be still." He spoke to the storm, and all of a sudden, everything was calm. There was not even a ripple on the water or a breeze. He asked His disciples, "Why were you so afraid? Do you still have no faith? You have heard all that I've said, and still you have no faith that God will protect you." How would you have felt? Would you have been afraid of sinking or drowning even though Jesus was in the boat with you?

The disciples looked at each other in amazement. They had been with Him when He performed miracles and had heard Him speak. Although they knew all this, they didn't realize that even the water and the wind would listen to Him. "Who was this man that even nature obeyed Him?"

Questions

Who was in the boat? (Disciples and Jesus)

Why was Jesus asleep? (He was tired.)

Why did the disciples wake Him? (They were afraid of drowning.)

Activity

Have children imagine they are in a boat. With chalk, draw a boat on the floor for them to sit in. Show them how to move side to side and back and forth as if riding the waves. Tell them to shut their eyes. Tell the story about the winds getting higher and the waves tossing them. Have the children move with the waves up and down, side to side, all the time using the rowing motion. Talk about the conditions, and when they're really feeling a part of the story, squirt them in the face with water. They will be shocked. I not only used a squirt bottle but also splashed water all over them—lots to clean up but fun.

Craft

Make the disciples' boat in the Sea of Galilee.

Instructions

Using a funnel, fill the bottle half-full with water. Add blue or green food coloring, small drops at a time, until it looks like the color of the ocean. Add one tablespoon of sand or glitter to each bottle. Using the funnel again, finish filling the bottle with cooking oil. Place a small boat or piece of wood to represent the disciples' boat inside. Apply glue to the outside of bottle and securely screw on top. You may apply an added ring of hot glue to prevent leakage. As the bottle is tilted from end to end, see how big the waves are and the trouble the boat has staying afloat.

Supplies

Bottles, green or blue food coloring, water, oil, funnel, sand or glitter, small boat or wood, and glue.

The Good Samaritan

Matthew 22:37–39; Luke 10:30–37

Jesus was speaking to a crowd of people when an expert on the law tested Him. He asked Jesus what the greatest commandment was. Jesus answered, "Love the Lord your God with all your heart and with all your soul and with all your mind. This is the first and greatest commandment. And the second is like it, Love your neighbor as yourself." Another man who appeared to also know the law asked, "What neighbor do you mean?"

Jesus told a story about a Jewish man traveling from Jerusalem to Jericho. The distance between these two cities was about seventeen miles and downhill all the way. It was a dangerous area where many travelers had been beaten and robbed. In this deserted area, the Jewish man was beaten, robbed, and left for dead by thieves.

A Jewish priest walking the same road saw the man lying on the ground, but did not stop, and only crossed to the other side. The next person seeing the man was a Levite, a person who was a leader of the Jewish community, and he too passed to the other side. Neither of them stopped to give help to the beaten man.

Another traveler riding a donkey saw the injured man and immediately got off his donkey to help the man. He was from Samaria, an area despised by Jews. Why was he helping a person he recognized as a Jew? No Jew had anything to do with anyone from Samaria, and the Samaritans had the same feeling toward the Jews. The Samaritan man had compassion for this injured man. He didn't even think about him being a Jew, only that he needed help.

After cleaning his wounds and pouring soothing oil on them, he lifted the man onto his donkey and walked with him to the nearest inn, which was like a motel. There he cared for him. When the Samaritan had to leave, he gave the innkeeper two silver coins and asked him to care for the Jewish man. He told the innkeeper that when he came that way again, if there was additional cost, he would pay. The two silver coins were enough to pay the man's bills at the inn for two months.

Jesus asked, "Of these three, who do you think was a neighbor to the man who was beaten?" The answer given was the one who had helped, the Samaritan. Jesus told the man to go and do the same for others, his neighbors.

Questions

How many people did not help the hurt man? (Two)

Who helped him? (A Samaritan)

How did he help? (He gave first aid and took him to the inn to recover.)

Craft

Make a Good Samaritan Kit for car or home.

Instructions

Provide each child with gallon-size Ziploc bag labeled "Good Samaritan." Have available various items for administering first aid such as Band Aids, antiseptic wipes, Kleenex, needle and thread, soap, etc. Collect many items, but let each child fill his or her own bag. Instruct the children to give the bags to their parents to always have supplies ready if needed, especially in their car.

Supplies

Individual purchased supplies as comb, Band Aids, and antibiotic cream, antiseptic wipes, Kleenex, wash cloth, needle and thread, scissors and hard candies. Emergency telephone numbers can also be supplied, but medicine packets should not be included.

The Prodigal Son

Luke 15

Jesus used parables, which are stories, when He taught the disciples and crowds. A favorite is in Luke 15 that tells of a wandering boy and the homecoming he received. This story is about love and forgiveness.

There was a wealthy Jewish man who had two sons. The older always worked hard and obeyed his father, but the younger was more carefree and liked to party.

One day, the younger son told his father that he wanted to leave home and travel. He persuaded his father to give him his inheritance, which was money he would receive if his father had died, and let him leave home. The father consented, and the younger boy left to a faraway land.

Have you ever had money to spend and spent it real fast? This is what happened to the boy. Soon, all his money was gone. He was far from home and hungry. He took a job feeding pigs, which was the worst thing a Jewish boy could do. Anything concerning pigs was considered unclean for the Jews, from eating them to just being around them. But there he was, pouring food, or "slop" as it often is called, to feed a bunch of pigs. Sometimes, he was so hungry that he may have eaten some of their food.

One day, he realized that the servants who worked for his father had easier lives than he did. They had food and clean clothes. The son decided to go home and ask his father to hire him as a servant.

Walking toward his home, he was scared and nervous. What if his father refused to let him come home because he had left and spent all his inheritance money?

Often, the father would look down the road, hoping one day he would see his son returning, and finally he did. He was so excited that he ran fast toward the boy. When he reached him, he grabbed him and hugged him tightly. The father had every right to disown the boy, but instead, he called to the servants to bring a robe, a ring which showed importance and wealth, and sandals. Since he had been a servant to the pig farmer, he had no shoes.

As they neared the house, the father told his servants to kill a "fatted" calf and prepare a feast. Tonight there would be a big party, music, and dancing because his lost son was home. This is not the homecoming the boy had expected. He had sinned against his father, but there was rejoicing when he returned home.

The older brother, coming in from working hard in the fields, heard all the music and saw the dancing. When he found out the party was for his younger brother, he was mad and told his father that it wasn't fair. He said, "I have worked hard, saved my money, and always did what you asked, but you wouldn't even let me have a goat, which was cheap, to party with my friends. Now, this foolish boy who left and spent everything came home, and you have given him a big party."

The father answered, "Son, you are always with me, and everything I have is yours, but now we have to celebrate. Your brother was dead, but now alive, was lost, but now is found."

This is the same way God acts when a sinner comes to Him. God rejoices, forgives, and loves him or her.

Questions

Why did the son leave? (He wanted to see other places and party.)

Was his brother mad when he returned? (Yes)

What did the father do when he saw the boy? (He ran to him, gave him new clothes, and rejoiced.)

Craft

Make a cardboard boomerang.

Instructions

Using poster board, cereal box cardboard, or heavy card stock, cut out a boomerang for each child using the template. Cut carefully and trim the rough edges. Fold slightly on each end where the solid lines are. If they are bent too much, the boomerang will not fly. Throw it like a Frisbee, by holding one of the arms on the side not bent. Twist your wrist toward your body, then toss it out. You may need to either bend the fold more or less. Keep trying. Children can paint or decorate, but remember that heavy decorations may hinder the flight.

The boomerang represents the Prodigal Son who returned to his father.

Supplies

Cardboard, boomerang template, scissors, and optional decorations.

Snack

Serve pig "slop" in individual bags. Mix chocolate pudding according to directions, dividing between bags. Place clean corn shuck to be used as a spoon. You may need extra spoons and Corn Bugles or corn nuts to serve with "slop."

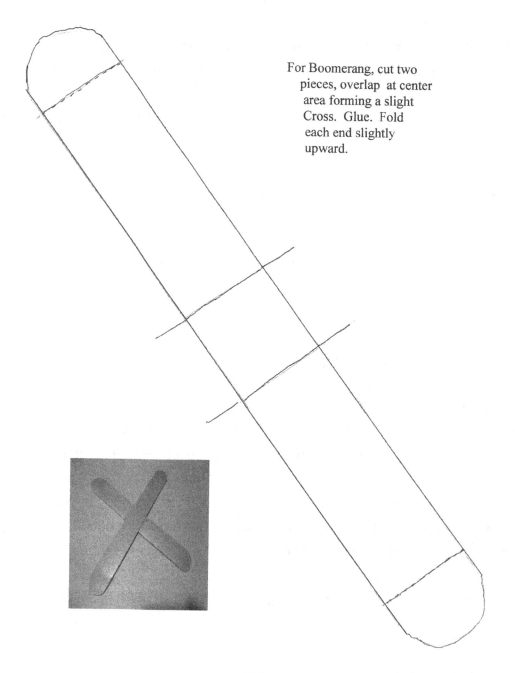

For Boomerang, cut two pieces, overlap at center area forming a slight Cross. Glue. Fold each end slightly upward.

Lazarus Come Forth

John 11:17–44

Lazarus, Mary, and Martha were good friends of Jesus who lived in Bethany, a town outside Jerusalem. Jesus had been in their home many times and often went there to rest and get away from the crowds.

Jesus was with His disciples when the message came that Lazarus was very ill. Mary and Martha knew Jesus healed many people and could make their brother well, so they sent for Him. After the messengers had traveled a day, they found Jesus and told Him of Lazarus. Knowing that Lazarus had died probably right after the messengers had left Mary and Martha, He said, "This sickness would not end in death, but that God's Son would be glorified through it." The disciples did not understand this, but they accepted His words.

After two days, Jesus told His disciples it was time to go to Bethany. The disciples reminded Him that only a short time ago the Jews wanted to stone Him there. They wondered why Jesus would return to Jerusalem. Jesus replied, "Our friend Lazarus has fallen asleep, and I am going to wake him." Thinking that Lazarus was better because of sleep, they didn't understand what Jesus meant. Jesus knew Lazarus had died and told them so.

After traveling for another day, they finally reached Bethany. When they arrived, they were told that Lazarus had died four days earlier and was already in the tomb. Several friends and Jewish leaders were with Martha when she saw Jesus coming. Martha ran to meet Jesus.

"Sir, if you had been here, my brother wouldn't have died, but I know that even now God will give you whatever you ask." She was hoping Jesus would perform a miracle and bring her brother back to life.

Jesus told her that her brother would rise. Martha said she knew that would happen on the last day, the one called resurrection day. Jesus said, "Do you believe that anyone who believes in Me, even though He dies, shall live again?"

She said, "Yes. You are the Messiah, the Son of God, and the one we have waited for." Jesus knew that she believed, but He wanted to hear her say it.

Martha went to find her sister. Mary was still at the house with friends who had come to comfort her. Martha told Mary that Jesus was there and wanted to see her. They both went to Him. All the friends followed, for they thought Mary was going to the tomb to mourn. They did not know Jesus had arrived.

Mary knelt before Jesus, saying, "Lord, if you had been here, my brother would not have died." Jesus saw her crying and He cried with her. The shortest Scripture in the Bible is John 11:35: "Jesus wept."

The friends and the Jews who had gathered felt compassion for Jesus and Mary, for they knew how much they had loved Lazarus. Others asked that since Jesus was the one who had healed the blind, couldn't He have saved Lazarus?

The tomb where they buried Lazarus was a cave with a big stone rolled in front. Arriving at the tomb, Jesus said, "Take away the stone." Martha told them that the smell would be terrible, for Lazarus had been dead for four days. Jesus did not respond. As the stone was rolled away, Jesus looked toward heaven and said, "Father, thank you for hearing Me." Jesus always knew God listened to Him, but He wanted these people to hear these words and believe He was God's son.

Very loudly, He said, "Lazarus come forth."

After a rustling noise inside the tomb, Lazarus walked out. He was still bound with the strips of material used for burial. Jesus said, "Unwrap him and let him go."

Lazarus was alive. Many had seen this miracle and finally believed Jesus was the long-awaited Messiah. They were very excited. Others saw what had happened and immediately ran to the Pharisees, who were trying to kill Jesus, and told them that Jesus was saying He was like God and could even raise the dead.

Which of the people seeing this miracle would you be like, the believers or the tattletale?

Questions

Who died? (Lazarus)

Where was Jesus when He heard Lazarus was ill? (Near Jerusalem)

What did Jesus say to Lazarus at the tomb? ("Lazarus Come Forth")

Craft

Make Lazarus Snacks for home.

Instructions

Give each child a plate, a wiener, and two strips of dough like biscuit or pie crust. Instruct them to place the wiener on the plate and using the strips of dough, bind the wiener, crossing over and around it. They are to take this wiener home with a printed instruction card telling how to cook it.

Activity

Choose two children to help, one to be Lazarus and the other the wrapper. Using an entire roll of toilet paper, the wrapper is to wrap and tightly bind Lazarus. Tell children this was the way people were prepared for burial. When finished, have all the children shout, "Lazarus come forth" as Lazarus walks and tears his bindings off.

Snack

Prior to the meeting prepare "Lazarus" snacks, one or two per child. Have juice and ketchup available. As they unwrap their snack to eat, say, "Lazarus come forth."

Supplies

Toilet paper, wieners, dough (crescent, pie crust, etc.), paper plates, juice, ketchup, and recipe card per child.

Card Instructions

Bake 350 degrees, 10 to 15 minutes. Cool and say, "Lazarus come forth" before eating.

Palm Sunday

Matthew 21:1–11; Mark 11:1–10; Luke 19:28–38; John 12:12–15

(This story is important for the children to hear because all four gospels tell of Jesus entering Jerusalem before the crucifixion.)

A week before Easter, on the day we call Palm Sunday, Jesus was approaching Jerusalem. He told his disciples to go into the city and find a colt, a young donkey, to ride. He said that if anyone asked them about it, say, "The Master needs the donkey." Jesus told them they would be allowed to take the colt. Horses were ridden by kings during war, but in peace times, the king would ride a donkey. Jesus was declaring himself a king. This entrance had been prophesized in Zechariah 9:9, "See the King comes to you, righteous and having salvation, gentle and riding on a donkey." The disciples didn't realize that this event was the fulfillment of that prophesy until after Jesus died.

The disciples spread their coats, their outer robes, on the donkey's back. They led it and Jesus into Jerusalem, shouting, "Hosanna! Blessed is He who comes in the name of the Lord." Many people in the crowd had seen Jesus perform miracles, and some had witnessed Lazarus walking out of the tomb. Also in this crowd may have been Bartimaeus, who had been healed of his blindness, the lady with the bleeding sickness, or perhaps some of the five thousand who had been fed. The popularity of Jesus was spreading. Jesus was their hero, their Messiah, and they saw Him riding on a donkey as a king, their king. This was the man who would save them, but the salvation Jesus would give was not from their Roman oppressors, as they hoped, but the gift of eternal life with God.

The crowds were great because Passover was approaching and many living outside of Jerusalem had come for the celebration. The excited crowd didn't know that in a few days, Jesus would be the sacrificial lamb offered for them. That day, they only felt the excitement of Jesus' coming to town.

They gathered on the streets. Some were waving palm branches, and some were laying their coats on the road. Excitement filled the air. For a short time, Jesus was treated like a king. Everyone was happy, except for the Pharisees who did not like that the people were giving Jesus so much attention. The Pharisees told Jesus to make the disciples and others be quiet, but Jesus refused. He said that if they kept quiet, even the stones on the road would burst out in cheers.

When Jesus entered Jerusalem, all the people of Jerusalem knew He had arrived. Those not knowing of Jesus were asking about Him, and many in the crowds answered, "This is Jesus, the prophet from Nazareth in Galilee. This is the Messiah." They felt that their long-awaited Savior had come.

On Palm Sunday, churches often celebrate by having children enter the sanctuary waving palm branches.

Questions

What was Jesus riding? (A donkey)

What did the people do? (Waved palm branches, put their robes on the road, and shouted, "Hosanna.")

Were the Pharisees excited like the people? (No, they told Jesus to keep the people quiet.)

Craft

Make cross pins for the congregation to wear for Palm Sunday.

Instructions

Cut two small strips of palm leaves to make a cross. Apply glue to the overlapping middle, and let dry before inserting the pin. These crosses can now be attached to a long straight pin to be passed out to the congregation during the children's message on Palm Sunday. Be sure to make enough for all the people in the congregation.

Supplies

Palm branches, scissors, glue, and long straight pins.

The Last Supper

Luke 22; John 13

Remember when the first Passover in the Jewish faith started? In the Old Testament, Moses appeared before Pharaoh and tried many ways to change the heart of Pharaoh and convince him to let the Israelites leave, but Pharaoh wouldn't change. Moses told the Israelites to take the blood of the lamb and splash it on their front door because that night, the angel of death would "pass-over" their homes when he saw the blood (Exodus 11:12). The death of the Egyptian firstborn was the last plague, and Pharaoh finally told Moses to take the Israelites and leave.

Each year, during the Festival of Unleavened Bread, Passover, the Jewish people eat a meal with several items such as bitter herbs, unleavened bread, and lamb to represent their former slavery to the Egyptians and how they had left so hurriedly. This is called a seder meal. Many churches today celebrate this meal on the Thursday before Easter.

The time had come for Jesus and His disciples to celebrate Passover. He told Peter and John to go into the city and prepare a place for them to have their meal. He said that when they entered the city, they would see a man carrying a jar of water and were to follow him. He would take them to a large upper room and for them to make preparations for their Passover meal. Peter and John followed His instructions.

During the meal, all the disciples were sitting or reclining on the floor around the table with Jesus in the middle. As Jesus was passing the bread and wine, He said the words that are used during Communion Service today. With the bread, He said, "This is my body given for you; do this in remembrance of me." Taking the wine, He said, "This is the cup of the new covenant of my blood poured out for you. Drink this in remembrance of me."

Later, Jesus said, "Tonight, one of you will betray me." The disciples looked around; they wondered to whom Jesus was referring. Jesus said, "The one who takes his bread and dips it into the dish." Judas Iscariot picked up the bread from Jesus, dipped it, and left the room. None of the disciples probably thought that Judas was the betrayer because he was the treasurer of the group, and during the celebration of Passover, money was distributed to the poor. They may have thought Judas had left to either purchase more food or distribute money. Jesus was the only one who knew the real reason why Judas Iscariot left the room.

After the meal was over, Jesus and the eleven sang a song and left the upper room. That was the last meal they would have together until after the crucifixion, but the disciples didn't know that.

Questions

Why were they celebrating? (Jewish traditional holiday, Passover)

What did they have to eat? (Bitter herbs, bread, wine, etc.)

Who took bread from Jesus and betrayed Him? (Judas Iscariot)

Activity

Enjoy a traditional Seder meal, the name of the meal the Jewish people eat during Passover to remind them of the leaving Egypt.

Instructions

Have all children sit or recline on the floor. As each food is passed, encourage each to taste it as the meaning of each is explained. Tell them that Jewish people still celebrate the Passover with the traditional foods.

Matzo—Flat, unleavened bread made with no yeast because they left in a hurry and the bread didn't have time to rise. Matzo can be purchased, or use flour tortillas.

Bitter herb—Parsley, which is similar to the hyssop bush used to paint the door with the lamb's blood so the angel of death could "pass over" their homes. The parsley can also be dipped in vinegar as was given Jesus on the cross.

Salt water—This is used to dip the herb in. This helps people remember the tears of the Hebrews in slavery and of crossing the Red Sea.

Lamb bone—This is a reminder of the lamb sacrificed at the first Passover. If a lamb bone is not available, use as an example any large bone from another animal except pig.

Egg—The egg represents the life of every Hebrew firstborn saved when the last plague was given and the Egyptian firstborn were killed.

Haroset—(Kha-row-st) This is a mixture of diced apples, nuts, and cinnamon as a reminder of the clay the Hebrews used to make bricks when slaves.

Any other food may also be used for a snack, but only after encouraging children to taste and hear the meanings of these.

Supplies

Flat bread, parsley, juice (wine), and a bone from a "lamb," boiled eggs, haroset, salt water, plates, cups and napkins, and optional additional snacks.

Dirty Feet

John 13:1–17

Jesus and His disciples gathered to celebrate the traditional Passover meal. He had been with His disciples for three years and had grown to love and care for all of them. Soon, He would be returning to His Father, but there was more to teach these men. He was their Master and Teacher. His responsibility was to prepare them for their future.

Jesus took off His outer robe, got a bowl of water and a towel, and knelt down before each disciple and washed his feet, one at a time. They were shocked. Although their feet were dirty because all wore sandals and the roads were dusty, the job Jesus was performing was that of a servant, not a Master. At that time, they had no servants, and no one in the group had volunteered to do this necessary job. Also, Jesus was doing this task during the meal, not before it, when foot washing was normally done upon entering a household.

Only Peter spoke about this. When Jesus knelt before Peter, he said, "Master you shouldn't be washing my feet." Jesus told him that one day he would understand the reason for it. Peter said, "No, Jesus, you should not wash my feet!" Why was Peter acting like that? Was he embarrassed because Jesus was his Master, not a servant, and that was a servant's job?

Jesus said, "Peter, you will never belong to me unless I do this!"

Peter consented. He told Jesus to wash his hands and his head too. Jesus said that one who bathed is already clean and only needs his feet washed to be entirely clean. Jesus looked around and said, "But that isn't true of everyone here." Jesus already knew one would betray Him, and that is what He meant when He said not everyone was clean. The others did not understand this statement.

Later, they learned that Judas Iscariot was the unclean person Jesus had referred to because he betrayed Jesus for thirty pieces of silver.

After completing the foot washing, Jesus put His robe back on and sat with the disciples. He started to explain His actions of washing their feet. He told them they called Him "Master" and "Lord," and that was true. He was their Master and had washed their feet, thus serving them. Now, they should serve others. No servant is greater than his master, and no messenger is greater than the One who sent him. He told them that knowing how to serve other people is a blessing.

As a Christian and followers of Christ, we are also called to serve. There are many ways that children your age can serve. Can you think of some? What about turning off lights in the church after leaving a room, picking up trash outside without being told, calling someone and checking on them, writing a care note, or just smiling when you see someone frown? We all can be servants to someone.

Jesus washed the dirty feet of His disciples and showed them that everyone can perform a task of serving, even the Son of God.

Questions

What did Jesus do? (He acted as a servant by washing the disciples' feet.)

Why didn't Peter want his washed? (He was embarrassed because Jesus was his Master.)

Who did Jesus say to serve? (Everyone)

Activity

Wash each other's feet.

Instructions

Have the children partner up; each partner is to wash the other's feet. Tell the first foot washers to remove their partners' shoes and socks and put one foot at a time in the basin. Wash by pouring water over each foot and then drying.

Have them switch places so the partners can wash their feet. See if someone will take the true role of a servant and wash the teachers' feet. This can be very meaningful or comical depending on the age of children. Embarrassment may also be involved, so be ready to emphasize why Jesus did this job.

Supplies

Several bowls of water and towels for the pairs to use.

The Path to the Cross

Matthew 27; Mark 15; Luke 22–23; John 18–19

The Jewish people were required to follow the laws given to Moses. The Sanhedrin, which was made up of the elders and priests of the temple, would often correct and punish the people for not obeying all the laws.

Jesus was becoming too popular with the crowds, and people were following Him and no longer listening to the Sanhedrin, which was trying to get rid of Jesus. If the Sanhedrin could convince the Romans that Jesus had done something against the Roman rule, He would be found guilty and be put to death by the Romans. His death would be the fault of the Romans, not the Sanhedrin. Later, one of the disciples named Judas Iscariot was part of this plan.

Jesus had been with His disciples enjoying the Passover meal, part of the Jewish celebration. All Jewish people had gathered for this festival. Because Satan had entered Judas Iscariot, he went to the chief priests and elders to discuss ways to betray Jesus. They gave Judas thirty pieces of silver. He had already left the disciples, but he knew where Jesus would be and was going to lead the soldiers to Him.

Later that night, Jesus went with to pray at a place called Gethsemane. The disciples with Him, were tired from their long day and soon went to sleep. Suddenly, a group of soldiers, elders, and priests approached the disciples. Judas had told them he would kiss Jesus on the cheek so they would know whom to arrest. When Judas went up to Jesus, He said, "Rabbi," and kissed Him. The soldiers immediately grabbed Jesus. Peter drew a sword and cut off the ear of one of the high priest's servants. Jesus said, "Put your sword away," and touched the servant. The ear was immediately healed. He asked the soldiers and priests why they had come at night to arrest Him when they were present when He was in the temple teaching and praying. No one answered as they led Him away to the house of the high priest. Most of the disciples ran away, but Peter followed at a distance.

When Jesus was arrested and later beaten, Judas felt bad. After hearing that Jesus would be killed, Judas tried to give the money back, but the elders would not take it. He ran away and hanged himself because of his shame. The elders used the thirty pieces of silver to buy cemetery land to bury strangers who died while visiting Jerusalem.

Pilate, the Roman governor, presided at Jesus' trial. He didn't want to condemn Jesus. When he found out that Jesus was a Galilean and under Herod's rule, he made a plan to send Jesus to Herod. Herod only mocked Jesus and returned Him to Pilate.

Pilate had to make a decision. Knowing the Jewish custom of releasing a prisoner during Passover, he asked the people to choose, maybe secretly hoping they would choose Jesus, between Jesus and Barabbas, a well-known criminal. Jeered on by the priests, the crowd chose Barabbas to be released.

When Pilate asked what he was supposed to do with Jesus, the people shouted, "Crucify him!" Pilate called for a basin of water and a towel. In front of all the people, he washed his hands and said, "I am innocent of this man's blood. It is your responsibility."

They took Jesus to crucify Him. Again, they beat Him and put a red robe and a crown of thorns on His head. (Bring a thorny branch like a holly or a mock orange for children to feel.) The crown was pushed down so tight that blood was dripping from His face.

Jesus had to walk to Golgotha, the place where He would be crucified. According to Roman custom, He would have to carry His cross along the path, which was crowded with many people. Being weak from the beatings, Jesus began to stumble. A man in the crowd, Simon of Cyrene, had come to Jerusalem for Passover. The centurion noticed Simon and motioned for him to carry the cross.

Nails were driven in the hands and feet of Jesus. (Show large nails to the children as examples.) Again, Jesus was mocked, this time by the elders and soldiers. Jesus was bleeding and hurting. When He asked for water, they gave Him vinegar to drink. (Let the children taste vinegar or just smell it.)

Later, when Jesus died, the sky turned dark, and the earth began to shake, and rocks fell. The people started to run away. When the curtain in the temple covering the Holy of Holies, an area never seen by common people, ripped apart from top to bottom, the people were scared. Graves opened, and dead people began to walk around. There was total destruction and chaos everywhere. Jesus, the Son of God, was dead.

The centurion who had been with Jesus throughout the trial and torture looked to His body on the cross and said, "Surely this man was the Son of God."

Questions

Why did the Sanhedrin want to kill Jesus? (They thought too many people were listening to Jesus instead of them.)

Who betrayed Jesus? (Judas Iscariot)

When Jesus died, what did the centurion say? ("Surely this man was the Son of God.")

Craft

Make a crown of thorns.

Instructions

Prior to class, purchase brown Play-Doh or mix one can yellow, one can red, and half a can blue Play-Doh to form brown Play-Doh. Cut sharp, pointed toothpicks into halves, enough for each child to have several. Tell the children they are going to make the crown of thorns.

Show children how to roll two long coils of Play-Doh and then twist them together to form a circle. Placing the circle on a plate, stick toothpicks into it, forming the crown of thorns. The toothpicks will be removed later, so "wiggle" them a little when inserting for easier removal. Tell the children to take their crowns home, and the only way they will be able to take the thorns out is by performing a good deed for someone. They are to report next week some of their deeds.

As the child explains to parents the crown of thorns, they can remove the thorns from their crown by their actions, but emphasize the pain Jesus had to endure on the cross.

Supplies

One can blue, yellow, and red Play-Doh, or brown, sharp toothpicks, scissors, and sturdy paper plates.

Snack

Serve round cookies spread with peanut butter or icing and circled with broken pretzels to represent the crown of thorns and red drink to represent the blood Jesus shed for them.

I Don't Know This Man

Matthew 26:31–75; Mark 14:27–28; Luke 22:30–34; John 18:25–27

Simon was one of the first disciples chosen to follow Jesus and one of those closest to Him. Jesus knew Simon's strength of character, and at the beginning of His ministry, Jesus changed Simon's name to Peter, meaning "the rock."

Jesus was enjoying the Passover meal with His disciples and started telling them that He would soon be leaving them. Using prophesy from Zechariah 13:7, He said that when their shepherd left, they would scatter. Peter said, "Even if all fall away on account of you, I never will fall away."

Jesus said, "I tell you the truth, this very night before the rooster crows, you will disown me three times." What does *disown* mean? Did Peter understand what Jesus was saying? No. Jesus told Peter that he would deny knowing Him not one time but three times. Peter did not believe Him.

After the meal, Jesus went with the disciples to the garden of Gethsemane. That was where Judas Iscariot led the soldiers, priests, and elders to arrest Him. Jesus was taken away to the home of the high priest, where he was laughed at, spat on, and beaten.

In the early morning before sunrise, the trial took place. News had spread about the arrest of Jesus, and a crowd gathered to watch the trial. Peter was among them. The high priest Caiaphas, of the Sanhedrin, the rulers of the Jewish people, and all the court officials were at the trial. Jesus, who had done no wrong, was on trial. Many of the rulers were witnessing against Jesus. Peter just watched in silence.

A girl said to Peter, "You were with that Nazarene." Remember Jesus was from Nazareth. Peter said that he didn't know what she was talking about and moved to another place to watch.

The girl told those around her, "He is one of them," probably pointing to Peter. Again Peter denied it, meaning he wasn't a follower of Jesus.

Some people told Peter, "Surely you are one of them. You are a Galilean."

Peter said, "I do not know this man you are talking about."

How many times had Peter denied knowing Jesus? (Three) Then Peter heard a rooster crow. Usually the roosters crow at early morning, so it had been a long night. During that night, Peter had denied knowing Jesus just as Jesus had predicted at the meal.

Then he heard the rooster crow again. Peter remembered the words of Jesus, "Before the rooster crows twice, you will deny me three times."

Realizing what he had done, Peter fell to the ground and cried. He knew what Jesus had said to him had come true. He had denied ever knowing his best friend three times.

Questions

What meal were Jesus and the disciples celebrating? (Passover)

What happened to Jesus while praying in the garden? (He was arrested.)

How many times did Peter deny knowing Jesus? (Three)

Craft

Paint a plaster rooster or make a bookmark with a rooster charm.

Instructions

Paint a rooster statue with acrylic paints. Have pictures available for examples of colors. For the bookmark, using thirty inches of ribbon or yarn, thread rooster charm on it. Secure the charm with a knot and then tie three additional knots at different intervals to show the number of times Peter denied knowing Jesus.

Supplies

Per child: rooster statue, acrylic paints, paint brushes or yarn or ribbon, and rooster charms. The plaster statues and charms can be purchased at craft stores such as Hobby Lobby or Michaels or at the craft section of a Walmart.

Jesus Is Alive

Matthew 28; Mark 16; Luke 24; John 20

The disciples watched as their Master hung on a cross, dying like a criminal. Jesus was not a criminal; He was the best person who ever lived. He was God's Son, and they all knew it.

As Jesus took His final breath, John, the beloved disciple, and Mary, the mother of Jesus, stood nearby. The sky turned dark, and the earth shook. Jesus was dead. When the soldiers lifted him down, Mary cradled Him tenderly, crying and holding Him close to her body. She and John walked slowly away after the guards made her leave.

A rich man and a follower of Jesus, Joseph of Arimathea, had asked Pontius Pilate if he could remove the body for burial in a tomb he had chosen for himself. Permission was granted, and Jesus was hurriedly taken to a tomb to be buried because the Sabbath was approaching. After placing Jesus inside, a huge rock was rolled over the entrance. Guards were placed on each side of the rock so no one would disturb it.

Early in the morning after the Sabbath, Mary Magdalene and two other women went to the tomb. They carried spices to anoint Jesus' body. Along the way, they were concerned about rolling the heavy rock away. As they neared the tomb, they realized that was not a problem. The rock was gone, the guards were asleep, and a white light came from inside the tomb. Looking in, they saw an angel standing near the place where Jesus' body had been laid.

"Do not be afraid," the angel said. "The one you are looking for is alive, just as He said He would be." The angel told them to go tell the others that Jesus would meet them in Galilee. The women were still frightened because of what they had seen, but they were very excited after hearing the angel's message. Suddenly, Jesus was in front of them. He told them the same thing the angel had said, to meet Him in Galilee. Jesus was alive! He had risen! What great news for all the believers. The women hurriedly left to find the disciples.

When the guards realized that Jesus' body was gone, they went to the chief priests and told them what had happened. The Jewish leaders offered them a bribe to not tell the truth but to say that the disciples had stolen Jesus' body. They accepted the bribe. Even today, many Jews do not believe the resurrection of Jesus. This story is told in all four gospels, each a slightly different way. However, the main point is that Jesus was no longer dead but alive again!

Jesus had lived, walked with His disciples, healed many people, was crucified, buried, and had risen from the grave. He would stay on earth for about forty more days before leaving to live with God. When He left for the final time, He promised the disciples, "I will be with you always even to the end of the world." This same promise applies to us now. He is up in heaven still watching and caring for us.

Questions

Who did the women see in the tomb? (Angels)

Why were the women going to the tomb? (To put spices on the body)

What happened to Jesus? (He rose from the grave and lives.)

Craft

Prepare and eat Resurrection Rolls

Instructions

Demonstrate the following recipe:

Canned biscuits enough for each child to have one or two

6 tbs. sugar

1 tsp. cinnamon

1/4 cup melted butter

Flatten out biscuit dough into circle. Place a marshmallow in center, pinching and folding dough closed. Dip the top in butter and then in the sugar, cinnamon mixture. Bake for 10 to 15 minutes at 350 until golden brown. Do not over bake. Serve as snack.

The children will experience the disappearance of Jesus from the tomb just as the marshmallow disappears.

Supplies

Canned biscuits, sugar, cinnamon, marshmallows, oleo, oven, and paper plates.

Optional

Color the picture of the angel in the tomb.

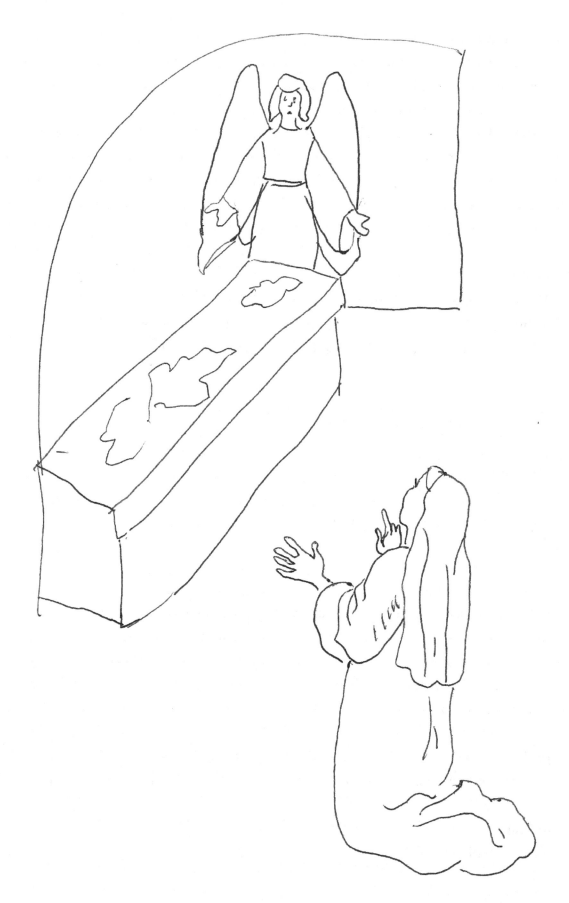

Doubting Thomas

Luke 24:36–38; John 20:19–29

Ten of the disciples were gathered in a locked room during the next week after Jesus' crucifixion. Those missing were Judas Iscariot, who had betrayed Jesus, and Thomas. The disciples were meeting in secret because they feared the Jewish authorities would hurt them as they did Jesus. Suddenly, Jesus was standing in the middle of the group. They were shocked. Was this a ghost, or were they really seeing Jesus?

Jesus said, "Why are you troubled and why do doubts rise in your minds? Look at my hands and feet. It is I myself. Touch and see; a ghost does not have flesh and bones, as you see I have" (Luke 24:37 NIV). Their Jesus was alive and really with them. How excited they were. He then asked for something to eat and was offered some fish. Sitting and talking with them, Jesus said just as His Father had sent Him, they would also be sent, but He did not say where. They were to be witnesses of Jesus, but they were to stay in Jerusalem until the Spirit came to them. The disciples didn't understand, but they would obey Jesus.

Jesus left as quickly as He had come. Later, when these disciples saw Thomas, they told him about seeing Jesus. Thomas didn't believe what they said. He said, "Unless I see the nail marks in His hands, and touch them, and feel the sword mark in His side, will I really believe that He lives."

A week later, all eleven, including Thomas, were in the upper room behind locked doors. Suddenly, Jesus stood in the middle of the group. "Peace to you," He said. When Thomas saw Him, he started backing away. He was scared. He had seen Jesus die, so how could this be His Master whom he loved?

Jesus told Thomas, "Thomas put your finger here; see my hands. Reach out your hand and put it into my side. Stop doubting and believe" (John 20:27 NIV). Jesus then told him, "Because you have seen Me, you believe, blessed are those who have not seen and yet have believed." Thomas did as Jesus told him, and then knelt down and said, "My Lord, my God."

Sometimes, all of us are like Thomas. We have to experience something to know it is real. We can't touch the sun, but we feel its heat. We can't touch the wind, but we can see the trees blowing. We can't see God, but by reading and studying our Bible, we know He is real. We don't have to touch to believe.

The Bible tells us stories about Jesus, and often in our imagination, we can experience the same things He did. Thomas had to feel Jesus to know He was really alive, but our faith in Jesus and God will tell us He is real. Jesus promises special blessings to all who believe even though they have not seen.

Questions

How many disciples were in the group when Jesus first appeared? (Ten; Thomas and Judas Iscariot were missing.)

Why didn't Thomas believe? (He had seen Jesus die but had to touch the nail holes to believe.)

Did Jesus appear to the group again? (Yes, and Thomas was with them and believed.)

Craft

Make a balancing bee. Say: "Do you believe I can balance a piece of paper on my finger?" Do you doubt me as Thomas did?

Instructions

Using cardboard, trace and carefully cut out the bee template, one per child. Let the children color the wings and body. Tape a penny to each end of the underside of the wings. The bee when placed on the finger will remained balanced. When this happens, ask the children why they had doubted.

Supplies

Bee template, two pennies per child, glue or tape, cardboard, crayons and scissors.

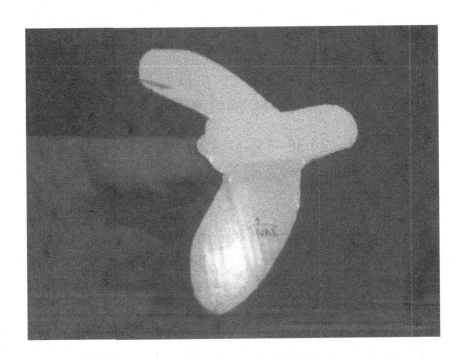

"Doubting Thomas"
Balancing Bee

Trace and cut one or two per child.

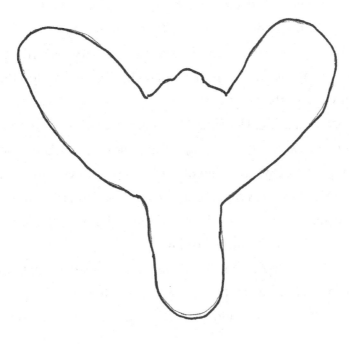

Ascension

Luke 24:50–53; Acts 1:1–11, 2:14–16

Jesus appeared to His disciples many times during the next forty days after the resurrection. There were ten or eleven times recorded in the Bible, and each time, the disciples were excited and eager to listen to Him. Jesus was preparing them for their future after He was gone. They didn't realize He would leave them again. Once appearing behind closed doors, He proved to all He was really alive. Remember that Thomas was not with them the first time and did not believe Jesus was alive. He had to touch the nail holes in Jesus' hands to believe.

Another time, Jesus appeared when all the disciples were out fishing, He called to them as He was preparing their breakfast. As He visited with them, He gave further instructions for spreading His story.

The last time the disciples would see Jesus was near Bethany, the city mentioned in the story of Lazarus. The disciples wanted to know when God was going to make Israel into the powerful nation it once was. Jesus told them that only God knew that. He told them to return to Jerusalem and wait, for soon they would be baptized with the Holy Spirit who would give them the power to tell everyone about Him and His life. The message of the Great Commission found in Matthew 28:28 told the disciples they were to spread the gospel to all the world. Jesus ended this talk by telling them, "and surely I will be with you always, to the very end of the age."

When Jesus finished talking, He lifted His arms toward heaven and began to ascend into the clouds. They stood there for a long time looking toward the heavens. Jesus was gone. Two angels appeared, saying, "Men of Galilee, why do you stand there looking into the sky? The same Jesus who has been taken from you into Heaven, will come back the same way you have seen Him go into Heaven" (Acts 1:10 NIV). That prediction is one that Christians everywhere still wait for today.

Can you imagine the disciples' conversation as they headed back toward Jerusalem? Probably everyone was talking at the same time. All had seen the crucifixion and resurrection of their Master. They had seen Him appear and disappear through closed doors and out of nowhere. They had experienced yet another miracle of Jesus' life just then.

He had given them more instructions to carry His message to the world. Do you think they were scared? Or do you think they were still so excited about seeing Jesus again that they didn't even think of their future? They knew that Pentecost was approaching in ten days, but they didn't know how much their lives were going to change. They went to Jerusalem and waited.

Questions

How many times did the disciples see Jesus after His resurrection? (Several)

What did Jesus tell the disciples to do after He was gone? (Spread the gospel everywhere.)

Where did Jesus go? (He ascended into heaven.)

Craft

Using the flame of a candle, tell the story of the Holy Spirit and Ascension.

Instructions

Give each child a candle with a drip protector. These can be made by using a large circle or square of paper, cutting a small X in the center, and inserting the candle. After lighting them, dim the lights and again tell parts of the story. Remind them that Jesus is the light of the world. Tell about the disciples being baptized with the Holy Spirit and that the flame of the candle represents that. Blow out the candles and watch the smoke rise. Explain that this is the same way that Jesus ascended into heaven. Each is to take a candle home.

Supplies

One candle and drip protector per child, and matches.

Optional

Coloring sheet.

Go Into All the World

Acts 1–2, 6–8

After Jesus was taken up into heaven, the disciples returned to Jerusalem where they stayed until Pentecost, which was about ten days away. That was the time Jesus had told them to remain in Jerusalem. He said that John the Baptist had baptized people with water, and they too would be baptized, but it would be with the Holy Spirit. The disciples didn't really understand what Jesus was saying, but they loved Him and believed His words.

The disciples along with many other followers of Jesus met and decided to elect someone to take Judas Iscariot's place. They elected a man named Mathias. He was with the group as they were gathered in an upper room. Suddenly, a strong wind came through the room, and each disciple saw what looked like a flame of fire above each other's head. All of them were filled with the Holy Spirit, just as Jesus had told them. They began to speak different languages and made a lot of noise.

The crowds below heard the noise and wondered if they were having a party. Some of these people in the crowd had gathered for the festival of Pentecost, and some were just citizens living in the area. Peter stood at the window and explained to the people outside what was happening. He gave one of the longest sermons ever, telling the story of Jesus from the predictions of the prophet Joel. He said that the man they crucified was the awaited Lord and Christ.

Then the disciples dispersed among the people. They began witnessing, and Peter led the disciples, saying, "Repent and be baptized every one of you, in the name of Jesus Christ for the forgiveness of your sins. And you will receive the gift of the Holy Spirit." More than three thousand people were baptized.

These converts were later called Christians, and at that Pentecost, the early churches were being formed as these new believers would gather. This was part of what Jesus said about spreading the gospel to all the world, for there were many different areas represented when these people went home. The gospel would be spreading fast.

However, the rulers of the Sanhedrin were not pleased. They arrested and put in jail some of the disciples, now called "apostles," meaning ones who are sent. Finally they were released after severe beatings and told not to speak about Jesus. But the warnings and beatings did not stop them. They went on daily telling the good news of Jesus.

The disciples chose seven more to help them with the churches that were rapidly being formed. Among them was a young man named Stephen. Stephen was on fire for God and talked to everyone about Jesus. He gave a long speech before the Sanhedrin and even accused them of having Jesus murdered. The Sanhedrin became so upset that they had Stephen arrested and stoned to death, one of the forms of execution at that time.

A Roman soldier named Saul was present at this execution. As witnesses laid their coats at Saul's feet, which may have meant he was in charge of the affair, he watched the stoning of Stephen.

Later, Saul became more determined to get rid of as many believers as he could and led many soldiers in the persecution of Christians. All the believers, including the apostles, were scattered. Thus the message of Jesus would again be taken everywhere.

In the pursuit of more Christians, Saul traveled to Damascus. On the road, he had an encounter with Jesus, who appeared before him and asked why he was persecuting Christians. Saul was blinded for three days by a bright light, and then he was converted and baptized. He became one of the main missionaries who helped spread the message of Jesus Christ throughout the world. His name was changed from Saul to Paul, and his travels and ministry are told throughout the New Testament.

Questions

What happened at Pentecost? (The disciples were baptized with the Holy Spirit.)

Who was Stephen? (He was one of the seven chosen to help the disciples with the early churches.)

In Jesus' time, was it easy being a Christian? (No.)

Do you know how to ask Jesus into your heart? (This is where you give the plan of salvation and Scriptures to explain.)

Plan of Salvation (The ABCs backward)

C: Confess that you are a sinner. A child does not know sin, but explain this in their terms. Romans 3:23: "For all have sinned and fall short of the glory of God." (NIV)

B: Believe that God loves you. Ask if they believe in Jesus and that He was God's son. John 3:16: "For God so loved the world that He gave His only begotten Son that whosoever believeth in Him should not perish, but have everlasting life." (KJV)

Romans 5:8: "But God demonstrates His own love for us in this: While we were still sinners Christ died for us." (NIV)

A: Ask Jesus to come into your heart. This is simple, but often children as well as adults expect to be immediately changed. Explain to them that with Jesus in their lives, they will never be alone, and He will always be with them. Revelation 3:20: Jesus said, "Here I am! I stand at the door and knock. If anyone hears my voice and opens the door, I will come in."(NIV) Romans 10:13: "Everyone who calls on the name of the Lord will be saved." (NIV)

Additional Crafts and Activities

Bible Verse Frame

Supplies

Five wooden craft sticks, glue, scissors, construction paper, yarn, fine-line marker, and paper punch.

Glue the sticks in a house shape, overlapping edges to make frame.

Cut the construction paper to fit the house.

Write on the paper Joshua 24:15c. Punch hole in the top of the paper to aid in hanging. Decorate the frame and Scripture if desired.

Glue Scripture to back side of frame and let completely dry.

Insert yarn through the hole and over the frame, tying a bow.

Give as gift or hang in room.

> But for me
> And my household,
> We will serve
> The Lord.
> Joshua 24:15c

Christmas Bookmark

Supplies

Greeting cards, paper punch, and colored yarn.

Cut two strips from the greeting cards the length of card and two inches wide. Make wider if desired. With paper punch, make holes about a quarter-inch from the edges of strip all around the sides, gluing the first and last piece of yarn on backside.

Weave yarn through the holes on three sides, starting with the first hole on sides, leaving the bottom holes open.

In bottom holes, cut pieces of yarn five inches long, one for each hole. Fold yarn in half, forming loop in the top. Insert loop from the back side and pull the loose ends through loop, tightening to form fringe. Repeat in all holes.

Make several to give to homebound persons or friends.

Tissue Paper Art

Supplies

Wood picture frame, wood box, glass figurine, votive cup, or any object to "paint" with tissue paper, various colors of tissue paper, and white glue or Mod-Podge. The glue may have to be thinned with water.

If using wooden object, first spray with white paint and let dry.

Cut or tear small pieces of paper, and glue on, overlapping the edges.

With thinned glue or Mod-Podge, seal the entire area. Let dry.

Finger Paint

Using any non-menthol men's shaving cream and a Formica-style table top, give children an ample supply of the shaving cream and let them "finger paint." This is a good way to clean the tables after an art project.

Have paper towels and wet cloths for cleanup. This is just another art medium to use.

Soap Bubbles

2 cups warm water

1 tbs. sugar

2 tbs. liquid detergent

1 tbs. glycerin (optional)

Combine ingredients. Glycerin will make bubbles iridescent. Blow bubbles through wire loops made with pipe cleaners. Outside, use "baby clothes" hangers or fly swatters in the soapy water and swing around. This is a cheap and fun activity.

Rock Paperweight

Supplies

Smooth rocks that have been washed and dried, metallic gold or silver spray paint, and permanent markers.

Spray the rocks with the metallic paint.

After completely dry, write a message from a Scripture from the Bible pertaining to rocks such as Deuteronomy 32:4, Psalm 89:26b, or 1 Corinthians 10:4.

Ask, "Why is Christ compared to a rock?" (Solid, strong, always there)

Example

Christ
Is the Solid
Rock of my
Life.

Additional Recipes

Cinnamon Christmas Ornaments

    1 cup ground cinnamon

    4 tbs. glue

    3/4 to 1 cup water

Prior to meeting, stir together glue, cinnamon, and water until it is the consistency of cookie dough.

Put clay in refrigerator for two hours until chilled. Remove and knead to make smooth ball.

For children: sprinkle dry cinnamon on work surface. Tell children to knead the clay until it is smooth and not sticky. You may have to sprinkle more cinnamon as they work.

Roll out and cut shapes. For ornaments, make holes in the top before setting to dry.

Air drying may take up to four days; the clay should be turned over daily to prevent curling. Can also be dried in warm oven for 1 ½ to 2 hours.

If not using clay immediately, store in plastic bag in refrigerator.

This recipe will make six to eight small or four large ornaments.

Baker's Clay

    4 cups flour

    1 cup salt

    1 1/2 cups water.

Mix and knead. Add more water if needed. Roll and cut into shapes with cookie cutters, or use free-form designs. Bake one hour in 300 degree oven until hard. After painting, spray with shellac. To keep dough fresh, keep in refrigerator until needed.

Cornstarch Clay

    1 cup salt

    1/2 cup cornstarch

    1/2 cup water

Mix and cook over low heat until mixture follows spoon and is stiff. Add a few drops of oil to prevent drying too fast. Let children free form shapes. Air dry for at least two days, turning daily. Can also be dried in oven for about one hour.

Edible Sugar Clay

    1 cup water

    2 cups sugar

    3 cups flour

Mix all together, and add a little more water if needed. Put flour on work surface. This dough can be used with cookie cutters, etc. It is not as durable as the salt dough, but it is edible. Air dry or oven dry on low temperature.

Creative Clay

    1 (1 pound) package baking soda

    1 1/4 cup cold water

    1 cup cornstarch

    Food coloring (optional)

Mix soda and cornstarch; add water. Cook and stir over low heat until consistency of mashed potatoes. Remove from heat and cover with damp cloth until cool enough to handle. Use for play dough or roll it out to make cookie shapes to decorate as ornaments for Christmas. Put hole in top before drying for hanging. Clay air dries very hard. Can be painted after drying.

Jell-O Jigglers

    1 1/2 cups boiling water

    2 (6 ounce) packages of Jell-O gelatin, any flavor

Stir boiling water into dry gelatin and mix in large bowl until completely dissolved. Pour into 13" x 9" pan. Refrigerate at least three hours until set. Cut into shapes or squares. Makes twenty-four servings.

Pretzels

Pretzels were formed as the arms and hands crossed in prayer. May be used at Easter.

2 cups all-purpose flour

1 package yeast

3/4 cup warm water

1 tbs. sugar

1 tbs. oil

1/2 tsp. salt (Kosher)

Dissolve yeast in water. Add the sugar, oil, and salt. Stir until mixed.

Knead and form into long coil and then into pretzel shape, folding ends over as praying arms. Brush tops with beaten egg and sprinkle with coarse salt.

Bake ten minutes in a 425-degree oven.

Matzo or Passover Bread

2 cups flour

1 1/2 tsp. salt

1 tbs. cold butter or margarine

1/2 cup cold water

Mix the flour and salt. Cut the butter into mixture with two knives or pastry cutter until the mixture resembles corn meal. Add the water and mix. Knead dough about ten minutes. Roll thin and cut into circles, placing them on greased baking sheets. Place another sheet on top to prevent curling while baking. Bake at 375 degrees for twenty minutes. Remove and cool on wire rack. Serve with the Seder meal.

Jewish Haroset or Charoset

6 apples peeled, cored, and chopped

1 cup finely chopped walnuts

1 tsp. cinnamon

1 tbs. white sugar

1 tbs. honey
1/3 cup red wine or apple or orange juice

Combine walnuts and apples, sprinkle with cinnamon and sugar. Mix honey with wine or juice and toss with the apple-walnut mixture. Refrigerate to be served with the Seder meal.

Glossary

Aaron: Brother of Moses. At age eighty-three, he crossed the Sinai Desert to stand with Moses to face Pharaoh.

Abel: Younger son of Adam and Eve who was killed by his brother, Cain.

Abednego: One of the youths captured with Daniel by the Babylonians. He was put in the fiery furnace with Shadrach and Meshach.

Abraham: Known as the first patriarch of Israel. God promised him as many descendants as there were stars.

Adam: First man God created.

Ahab: Eighth king of Israel who reigned for twenty-three years in Samaria.

Angels: Messengers from God.

Apostles: Disciples chosen by Jesus who were sent with a special mission. Peter, James, John, Andrew, Phillip, Matthew, Judas Iscariot, James the Less, Thomas, Simon the Zealot, Bartholomew or Nathaniel, and Jude or Thaddeus.

Ascension: The ascent of Christ into heaven on the fortieth day after Easter.

Baal: A common name for the chief main god worshipped by the Phoenicians.

Babel: Meaning "confusion." The Tower of Babel was the building built to become the symbol of their God-defying disobedience and pride.

Balaam: A heathen diviner in Pethor who possessed some knowledge of the true God. He acknowledged that his superior powers were derived from God.

Baptism: Applying water as a rite of purification or initiation. Outward sign of follower of Jesus.

Beatitudes: Supreme blessedness or happiness in the nine declarations by Jesus on the Sermon on the Mount. (Matthew 5:3–11)

Belshazzar: the last sovereign of the Neo-Babylonian Empire.

Benjamin: Youngest son of Jacob and second son of Jacob and Rachel.

Bethel: A town about twelve miles north of Jerusalem; its name means "House of God."

Bethlehem: A town in Palestine where Jacob buried Rachel. Also called the City of David, as David had been born and anointed there. Also, the birthplace of Jesus.

Bible Books of Gospels: (4)—Matthew, Mark, Luke, and John.

Bible Books of History: (12)—Joshua, Judges, Ruth, 1 and 2 Samuel, 1 and 2 Kings, 1 and 2 Chronicles, Ezra, Nehemiah, and Esther.

Bible Books of Law: (5)—Genesis, Exodus, Leviticus, Numbers, and Deuteronomy.

Bible Books of Major Prophets: (5)—Isaiah, Jeremiah, Lamentations, Ezekiel, and Daniel.

Bible Books of Minor Prophets: (12)—Hosea, Joel, Hosea, Obadiah, Jonah, Micah, Nahum, Habakkuk, Zephaniah, Haggai, Zechariah, and Malachi.

Bible Books of Poetry and Wisdom: (5)—Job, Psalms, Proverbs, Ecclesiastes, and Song of Songs.

Boaz: A wealthy kinsman of Elimelech, the husband of Naomi. He later married Ruth.

Caesar: Name given or taken by all the Roman emperors after Julius Caesar. A title like Pharaoh.

Cain: Firstborn of the human race to Adam and Eve and also the first murderer.

Caiaphas: The high priest of the Jews present at the beginning of Jesus' ministry and at Jesus' condemnation and crucifixion.

Canaanites: Canaan was the fourth son of Ham, one of Noah's sons. The land named for his descendants.

Covenant: A binding agreement made by two or more parties, as God with Noah, and God with Abraham.

Daniel: Name means "God is my judge."' Hebrew prophet during the Babylonian captivity. Author of book of Daniel in Old Testament.

David: Israel's most famous king. Jesus is from the house of David

Egypt: Country where Joseph, Mary, and Jesus fled to when Herod was killing the baby boys.

Elijah: A prophet who may have been a recluse; he appeared only to deliverer a message from God, enforce miracles, and then disappear for a while. Was not buried but taken up to heaven in a fiery chariot.

Elizabeth: Mother of John the Baptist.

Eve: Name given by Adam to the first woman, his wife.

Ezekiel: Major Hebrew prophet of the sixth century and author of Book Ezekiel.

Gentiles: Meaning "foreigners"; name given to those not Jews in the New Testament.

Gideon: Judge of Israel and conqueror of the Midianites.

Goliath: Champion of the Philistines who died by the hand of David.

Gospels: Means "God messages." The first four books of the New Testament—Matthew, Mark, Luke, and John.

Hagar: Handmaid of Sarah, who was the mother of Ishmael with Abraham.

Hannah: A barren woman who prayed earnestly for a son. God granted that with birth of Samuel.

Hebrew: The first person who was called a Hebrew was Abraham. Name interchanged with Israelites. Descendants through Isaac and Jacob known as Hebrews.

Herod: Not a personal name but a family or surname. All generations of the Herodian house.

Isaac: Only son of Abraham and Sarah.

Isaiah: Greatest of the Hebrew prophets.

Ishmael: Eldest son of Abraham and Hagar born when Abraham was eighty-six.

Israel: The name given to Jacob who became the father of the twelve tribes of Israel.

Jacob: Second born son of Isaac and Rebekah. God changed his name to Israel. Father of the twelve tribes.

Jehovah: The name of God most frequently used in the Hebrew Scriptures of the Old Testament.

Jeremiah: Major prophet of the six and seventh centuries BC.

Jerusalem: Called the Holy City for Christians, Jews, and Islam. It is fourteen miles from the Dead Sea and five miles from Bethlehem. Capital of ancient and modern Israel regarded as holy by the Christians, Jews, and Moslems.

Jesus: Expected Messiah in the Old Testament. Son of God

Jethro: A priest or prince of Midian, the father-in-law of Moses.

Jonah: Fifth minor prophet born from the tribe of Zebulun. He disobeyed God.

Jonathan: Son of Saul and best friend to David.

Joseph: (1) Oldest son of Jacob and Rachel; (2) Husband of Mary, mother of Jesus.

Joshua: Assistant and successor of Moses.

Lazarus: Friend of Jesus whom Jesus brought back to life.

Leah: Eldest daughter of Laban, who by deceit became the first wife of Jacob.

Lord's Prayer: Model prayer taught by Jesus. (Matthew 6:8–15)

Lord's Supper: Also called Communion with symbolism of the partaking of the body and blood of Jesus.

Lot: Nephew of Abraham, known for settling around Sodom and Gomorrah.

Meshach: Name given to one of the companions of Daniel who were trained as personal assistants to the king.

Messiah: Used as Christ in the New Testament. The Son of God.

Methuselah: Son of Enoch and grandfather of Noah. He lived to be 969 years old. Listed as oldest in the Bible.

Moses: The deliverer, leader, lawgiver, and prophet of Israel.

Naomi: Woman of Bethlehem in the days of judges; mother-in-law of Ruth.

Nazareth: The home of Joseph, Mary, and Jesus. Jesus was called a Nazarene.

Nebuchadnezzar: King of Babylon who destroyed Jerusalem and carried the Jews into Babylonian captivity.

Noah: Son of Lamech and tenth in descent from Adam. When he was 600, he entered with his three sons, Shem, Ham, and Japheth into the ark.

Passover: Celebrated as a remembrance of the angel of death passing over the homes of the Hebrews.

Peter: Simon, the son of Jonas from Galilee and one of Jesus' closest disciples.

Pharisees: A member of ancient Jewish sect that emphasized strict interpretation and observance of the Mosaic laws.

Pharaoh: Title given to Egyptian kings.

Philistines: One of the people of ancient Philistia often called boorish and barbarous.

Pilate: Roman procurator (leader) of Judea, present at trial of Jesus.

Plagues of Egypt: Ten plagues from Moses to the people of Egypt: blood, frogs, lice, flies, death of animals, boils, hail, locusts, darkness, and death of firstborn.

Priest: A minister of a non-Christian religion. In the Catholic Church, the second in command to the bishop.

Prophets: Spokesperson from God to man.

Rabbi: The ordained spiritual leader of the Jewish congregation.

Rachel: Youngest daughter of Laban and one of Jacob's wives.

Rahab: a woman of Jericho at the time of Israel's entrance into the Promised Land.

Rebekah: Daughter of Abraham's nephew Bethuel. Arranged marriage to Isaac.

Resurrection: A rising from the dead or returning to life.

Ruth: A Moabite who followed her mother-in-law, Naomi, back to Bethlehem and married Boaz.

Sabbath: Refers to the seventh day of the week that God set aside for rest.

Sacrifice: The act of offering something to a deity, to God.

Sadducees: A Jewish sect that retained the older written interpretation of Mosaic Law against the oral tradition and did not believe in the resurrection of the dead.

Salt: A seasoning that Jesus mentioned when He said, "You are the salt of the earth" (Matthew 5:13).KJV

Samaritan: Inhabitant of Samaria, a division of ancient Palestine despised by Jews.

Samuel: Son of Elkanah and Hannah born in response from her earnest prayers. Hebrew judge and prophet.

Sarah: Wife of patriarch Abraham. Her name "Sarai" was changed at the same time Abram's name was changed to Abraham.

Satan: The chief of the fallen spirits.

Saul: Son of Kish from the tribe of Benjamin. The first king of Israel.

Sermon on the Mount: Name given to a discourse Jesus gave to His disciples and a multitude on a mountain in Capernaum.

Seth: Third son of Adam. He died at age 912.

Shadrach: One of the Jewish captives carried to Babylon by Nebuchadnezzar.

Snake or Serpent: Figurative. Malice of wicked used to represent Satan in some texts.

Sodom and Gomorrah: Twin cities that exploded with salt and sulfur, causing fire and brimstone to rain down. Lot and family saved.

Solomon: King of Israel, son of King David. He was noted for his wisdom and his wealth; he wrote three books of the Bible.

Twelve Tribes of Israel: Jacob with Leah: Reuben, Simeon, Levi, Judah, Issachar and Zebulun. Jacob with Rachel: Joseph and Benjamin. Jacob with Bilhah, maidservant of Rachel: Dan and Naphatali. Jacob with Zilpah, maidservant of Leah: Gad and Asher.

Zechariah: Father of John the Baptist.

Bibliography

Bacher, June Masters. *"The Quiet Heart"*. Eugene, OR: Harvest House 1988.

Beegle, Shirley. *301 Creative Crafts*. Cincinnati: Standard Publishing. 1969

Carlson, Bernice Wells. *Make It Yourself: A Handicrafts for Boys and Girls*. Nashville: Abingdon Press. 1950

Clark, Silvana. *Everyday a Holiday*. Grand Rapids, MI: Revell. 2004

Cochran, Diane. *Stories to Tell and How to Tell Them* Mystic, CT: Twenty Third Publications. 2002

Halverson, Delia. *Children's Activities for the Christian Year*. Nashville: Abingdon Press. 2004

Holy Bible. King James Version. World Publishing Company.

Johnson, June. *838 Ways to Amuse a Child*. New York: Cramery Publishing. 1959

NIV Study Bible. Grand Rapids, MI: Zondervan. @1985, 1995, 2002

Reader's Digest *Who's Who in the Bible*. Reader's Digest. Pleasantville, NY. 1994

Vurnakes, Claudia. *The Great Bible Question and Answer Book*. New York: Playmore. 1995

Wiseman, Ann. *Making Things*. Boston: Little, Brown, and Company. 1967

But Jesus said, "Let the little children come to me and do not hinder them, for the kingdom of heaven belongs to such as these."

Matthew 19:14 NIV

Printed in the United States
By Bookmasters